THE
MODERN
ORACLE

LAURENCE KING

First published in Great Britain in 2021 by
Laurence King Publishing
an imprint of The Orion Publishing Group Ltd
Carmelite House, 50 Victoria Embankment
London EC4Y 0DZ

An Hachette UK Company

10 9 8 7 6 5 4 3 2 1

Text © 2021 Lisa Boswell
Illustrations © 2021 Apolline Muet

A CIP catalogue record for this book is available
from the British Library.

ISBN 978-1-78627-896-8

Printed in China by Everbest

Designer: Alex Wright
Copyeditor: Sue Lascelles
Proofreader: Rosie Fairhead

Laurence King Publishing is committed to
ethical and sustainable production. We are
proud participants in the Book Chain Project®.
bookchainproject.com

THE MODERN ORACLE

FORTUNE TELLING
AND DIVINATION FOR
THE REAL WORLD

LISA BOSWELL

ILLUSTRATIONS BY APOLLINE MUET

CONTENTS

INTRODUCTION: WELCOME TO YOUR FUTURE!

———

Since the dawn of time, humans have sought to predict the future. It seems almost natural that we would turn to fortune-telling to improve our lives and the lives of our friends, families and our wider community. Whether it is through reading the entrails of sheep (yes, people really did this) or interpreting the dreams of kings, we have always sought to gain divine guidance with the help of fortune-telling.

The word 'divination' comes from the Latin *divinare*, a verb that means to foresee or foretell. A diviner is, therefore, someone who can see future events before they take place. By using divination, a diviner can predict what might happen in the coming weeks, months or years, and give advice based on what they see.

The most famous diviners often held positions of authority and are considered by history to be somewhat special. Joseph, a biblical prophet, interpreted the dream of the pharaoh and, as a result, rose to become the Egyptian prime minister. In mythology, Graeco-Roman heroes often visited oracles or a sibyl before they embarked on their quests. John Dee, a sixteenth-century psychic and crystal scryer, was the tutor and adviser to Queen Elizabeth I.

These impressive figures might lead you to believe that you have to be specially gifted to be a diviner, but this is not the case. It is safe to assume that ordinary people have always practised divination. In fact, you've probably been practising divination yourself without even realizing it. Believe it or not, the following are all acts of divination:

FINDING WHITE FEATHERS: if you're one of the many people who view finding white feathers or other objects as being spiritually significant, you are practising a method of divination known as 'apantomancy'.

READING AT RANDOM: if you open a book, read a random passage and interpret this as a message from a higher being, you are inadvertently practising a method of divination called 'bibliomancy'.

ASSIGNING MEANING TO YOUR DREAMS: if you have ever changed your actions because of a dream, this makes you a dream interpreter.

You may assume that you have to be psychic to become a diviner, but as you can see, you can make divining a part of your lifestyle without doing anything out of the ordinary. Psychic ability is something that grows stronger with divination; divination is not something you practise just because you're psychic.

Anyone and everyone can be a diviner. The future is open to all of us, not just a select few. Like practising any new skill or hobby, all you have to do is take the plunge and commit to learning it. Some methods of divination require tools, but not all do. To be a diviner, you do not have to stock up on fancy card decks and crystals.

I come from a Romany Gypsy background and had diviners in my family. Because of this, I began practising divination at a very young age. Around the age of 7, I began to use my older sister's Tarot cards: I would sneak the deck out of her bedroom and perform readings. This went on until I turned 10 and my mother bought me my own cards.

Although I loved the Tarot, I became enchanted by divination systems that did not require tools. In Romany Gypsy culture, discussing our dreams with friends and family members is a daily occurrence. My relatives would even tell me about past dreams they had and how these eventually manifested in real life. For example, when I was a baby, my mother had dreamed that I had a third eye on the back of my head – my family interpreted this as a 'sign' that I would one day be a reader of fortunes.

Gypsies are very big on signs and we believe that God, the universe and the spirits send them to us frequently. For us, some methods of divination are not viewed as divination but as ways of life. An omen, a dream or a minor setback can have spiritual significance. Over the years, I have discovered what different symbols represent and learned how to interpret others for myself.

A lot of people, including you, know much more about divination than they think they do. All human cultures, not just Romany Gypsies, assign special status to symbols every day; for example, you probably already know that clovers symbolize good luck and that fir trees are associated with Christmas. You can use this sort of knowledge to interpret dreams, read signs and even predict the future based on the shape of clouds! You can get started with divination right now, today – you already have everything you need to begin making predictions.

Divining is a skill you can use to improve every area of your life's journey. Most people think of divination as something that uncovers their future in general. While this is true, you can also use fortune-telling to assist you in your relationships, wellbeing goals, career and anything else that is not up to par with how you envisioned your best life to be.

Divination is one of those rare spiritual practices that can help you tackle serious issues, but it can also provide a bit of entertainment. You can practise divination by yourself or with friends and family. Divining the future can be a fun experience, especially if you use the best method of divination for the job.

All forms of fortune-telling can be used for every area of your life, but some systems really come into their own if they are employed for a particular purpose. For instance, you can use Tarot cards for divining pretty much everything, but the most popular way to use them is for love readings. The Tarot system has been perfectly designed to answer any and all questions related to relationships. Another example is astrology. While the positions of the planets can reveal details about your life in general, you can also use astrology to help make better decisions with regards to health, fitness and lifestyle. This book will show you different systems of divination and teach you the best ones to apply to different areas of your life. Throughout I will introduce you to many different types of divination method and teach you the basic principles and practices, but also show which method is best suited to different areas of your life.

While working through this book, you will find that some methods of divination are better suited to you than others, and that is perfectly OK. Divination is personal and largely based on preference. What works for others may not work for you, but I recommend that you give all the systems a try. Most diviners give everything a bash at least once.

So, let's get started on the quest to become a diviner! May the spirit be with you throughout this journey and beyond...

GETTING STARTED:
DIVINATION 101

———

Before you get started, here are some useful things you need to know, along with answers to a few frequently asked questions.

WILL ALL TYPES OF DIVINATION
WORK FOR ME?

The methods for each type of divination system can vary across traditions, so I've focused on the most common and popular methods. I've also kept them simple for the beginner diviner. As you grow in skill and confidence, feel free to explore other methods. Divination is personal, so if you find an alternative method you prefer, go with it. Also, you may find you have an affinity for some methods of divination and don't get on with others, and that's perfectly OK. This book is intended to act as a useful introduction to the craft, but where you take your newfound divination skills is up to you.

DO SYMBOLS ALWAYS MEAN
THE SAME THING?

There is a lot of variation in symbol meanings and their interpretations. The methods, symbols and interpretations in this book predominantly follow the most universal meanings and my own Romany Gypsy tradition. Other psychics from different backgrounds may have different methods and interpretations. Meanings and interpretations can also be influenced by our cultural values and our own personal experiences. Because your background and experiences are different from mine, you may interpret symbols differently – and this is perfectly legitimate. In fact, I urge you to come up with your own interpretations as this can make your readings even more personal and accurate.

Your own culture, experiences and circumstances will always influence how you interpret symbols; for example, I always interpret rodents negatively because they are considered *marime*, or dirty, in Gypsy culture. You may not agree with that because you have had positive experiences with mice. So, if you do not resonate with some of my symbolic meanings, it is perfectly OK to assign your own according to your beliefs. This book aims to help you develop your psychic abilities and interpretation skills in order for you to become a confident and skilled diviner.

DO I HAVE TO LEARN DIFFERENT SYMBOLIC MEANINGS FOR EVERY METHOD OF DIVINATION?

You'll be pleased to know that you do not have to learn new meanings for every method of divination. The symbols listed at the back of this book (see pages 189–92) can be adopted for any fortune-telling system – from tea leaf reading to dream interpretation.

However, the methodology behind how you apply these symbols varies between divination systems. For example, in tea leaf reading you have to interpret the symbol in relation to the teacup. In Lenormand card readings, you have to interpret the cards in relation to the spread. So while the symbols in this book will give you the meanings, the individual chapters will help you to apply those meanings to the various fortune-telling systems.

DO I HAVE TO KNOW THE MEANING OF EVERY SYMBOL?

You do not have to memorize every single symbol to become a capable diviner. Instead, you should work on learning the most common symbol meanings. As mentioned, there are handy, simple reference guides at the back of this book to help you (see pages 189–92). The interpretations offered in the book are deliberately simplified and focused for newbie diviners, but as you learn more about divination and explore each method, you will develop a greater understanding of the symbols and will be able to give more nuanced readings.

HOW DO I KNOW WHICH MEANING TO USE?

A single symbol, card or crystal etc. can have multiple meanings. For example, in the divination system of Lenormand, the Fish card can symbolize money but also water or fluid. So, how do you know which meaning you should use?

When you interpret a symbol or card you will take a variety of factors into account. The question you're answering, the spread you're using, the positions the objects fall in, how the reading progresses and your intuition will all point you towards the right meaning.

Some meanings make more sense within the context of the reading. Most readings answer a specific question, so the type of question you're answering can lead you towards the correct meaning. If you're performing a business reading with a Lenormand deck, the Fish card is more likely to represent money than it is to symbolize water.

Other than the question, some divination methods require the use of spreads, which you'll learn about in Chapters 4 and 5 (the Lenormand and Tarot chapters), or boards, which you'll learn about in Chapter 13 on casting. Just as you will discover how to interpret the symbols with regard to the question, you'll also take the meanings of these positions into account. So, in a Lenormand Grand Tableau spread you'll find a position called the House of Clover, which represents luck. If your Fish card falls here, this card is more likely to represent money than it is to represent water, because good fortune often means an increase in wealth.

How your reading progresses and the combinations that arise can also give you clues as to the meaning of a particular card or symbol. If, in a Lenormand reading, you were to pull a Scythe or Coffin card (which can predict loss) and then the Fish card, this would most likely predict a loss of money. In itself, the Fish is usually quite a neutral card and is negative only when combined with a dire card, such as the Scythe, or positive only when combined with a good one, such as the Sun.

Finally, the most reliable way to interpret a symbol is to rely on your intuition. This will often lead you towards the right meaning. That is why the start of this book focuses heavily on intuitive and spiritual development. If all else fails, your intuition will lead you down the right path.

You should always treat your divination objects with special care, because doing so will ensure that you take your readings seriously. If you do not view your readings as important, you will not pay attention to what they tell you or take their advice, and you will not believe in your predictions.

If you assign spiritual significance to your divination objects, this will help you to see your readings through a sacred lens. Having a special care routine for your divination objects – such as keeping them in their specifically assigned space – can also help your readings become more ritualistic or ceremonial.

From the moment you assign something the role of 'divination object' you can start to perform readings with it. To create a strong bond with it, practise your readings often. To strengthen this bond with your new divination tool, you should keep it in close proximity to you. Carry it around with you for a few weeks. Place it on the nightstand next to your bed. Allow it to soak up your energy.

Most diviners feel that having a special place to store divination objects is imperative. You can wrap your divination objects in silk cloths or house them in drawstring bags. Some diviners keep their divination objects wrapped up and stored in wooden boxes. Personally, I prefer not to have my divination objects hidden away; I like to have them out in the open as I feel that makes them a bigger part of my life, but there are no hard and fast rules.

I am also of the opinion that you should not allow other people to touch your divination objects. Not letting any old person play with your tools will mean that your tools retain a meaningful connection to you and your life. They are yours and yours alone. I do not even allow my seekers to shuffle their own cards for card readings.

HOW TO WORK WITH THE ETHICS OF DIVINATION

There are many ethical concerns related to divination, especially when it comes to reading for other people. Everyone will have their own ideas about what constitutes ethical and unethical behaviour. You will find that ethics often differ based on each individual's religious, cultural and social background. Whether you agree or not with another diviner's ethics, it's important to be respectful of them. Here are a couple of areas to consider when it comes to the ethics of divination.

DOES DIVINATION TAKE AWAY MY FREE WILL?

No, divination does not take away free will. While there are things that are destined to happen (and are unavoidable), we always have a choice as to how we are going to get there.

Let's say that your divination has predicted that you and your friends are going to one day visit a river together. One of your friends walks to the river, but another drives. You hitchhike. You have all chosen how and when you visit the location using your own free will, but eventually, you all arrive as predicted.

Some aspects of life we can predict because they are meant to be, for whatever reason. Other aspects do not have far-reaching consequences for us, so we can sway them in a particular direction. As you step into the role of diviner, you will find it easier to spot the avoidable and unavoidable, but remember that this is something that comes with experience. For now, just worry about recording your forecasts for accuracy, and in the future you can look back on predictions you have experienced or avoided.

SHOULD I CONSIDER MY STATE OF MIND WHEN PRACTISING DIVINATION?

It is best if you perform your readings when you are in a steady emotional state. If you try to read cards, for example, straight after a break-up or argument you will find that your reading is much harder to interpret. When you're feeling as though you 'really' need an answer, it is probably best to wait until the next day when your emotions are stable and your interpretations objective.

CAN I READ THE SAME MATTER MORE THAN ONCE?

Do not form a habit of reading the same matter more than once, as doing so can cause you to become obsessive. While it can help you to navigate life, divination is not the answer to all your problems. You should record the results of your readings so that

you can refer back to them and
avoid reading on the same matter.

The exception to this rule is
that you can read the same matter
again if something has changed in
that situation – this is because, if
the circumstances have changed,
the situation has changed. For
example, if you have read on your relationship when you and your
partner were together but now you have separated, it is OK to
read the matter again, because your circumstances are different.

Similarly, it is OK to read on the same situation again if most
of your past reading has come to fruition. Once your initial reading
has played out, there is no reason why you cannot perform another
reading on the same matter. But, again, avoid reading on the same
matter if your reading has not had time to happen.

HOW OLD DO I NEED TO BE
TO PRACTISE DIVINATION?

Not only do some people think it is wrong to allow younger people
to read, but they also believe that you should not read for anyone
under the age of 18. However, there is nothing wrong or dangerous
about divination itself, and in my experience it's perfectly OK to
read for teenagers or younger children in your family.

In fact, reading for children and allowing them to read is a
good way to introduce them to divination from an early age. As
I've mentioned, I started practising divination at the age of 7.
People who start fortune-telling when they are young are at an
advantage when they become adults, because it is easier to learn
as a child than it is as an adult.

SHOULD I REVEAL EVERYTHING
I FORESEE TO THE SEEKER?

Where are the boundaries when we veer into the lives of our friends and family or strangers? Should we reveal everything we divine? Even when reading for yourself, it is difficult to predict everything that is going to happen with regards to your situation. There will be things that, for whatever reason, you cannot uncover. The same is true when it comes to reading for other people. I believe that if you're not meant to know something, it will not be revealed through a reading. What you receive is intended to be shared.

CHARGING MONEY FOR
YOUR READINGS

Another major ethical concern is whether or not it is wrong to charge money for a reading. Most diviners believe that it is not wrong to accept payment for readings, and divination has been a livelihood for many people for centuries.

It is common for diviners not to want to charge their friends and family members for readings. Who you charge for readings is a personal decision, and you may not even want to make money from divination. If you do accept payment for your readings, you will have to learn how to balance helping friends and family with reading for paying customers. You don't want to get taken advantage of. This balance gets easier to find with time.

HOW LONG SHOULD I WAIT BEFORE READING FOR OTHERS?

Some newbie diviners wonder if there is a set period of time that they should wait before they read for the next person. There are no hard and fast rules about how long you should be divining for before you start reading for seekers.

I do not believe that you should wait to read for other people. You can start reading for others as soon as you receive your divination objects. Reading for others will help you to gain experience and become a better diviner.

However, you may not want to charge money for your readings until you feel confident in your ability to make predictions and help potential clients. Again, there is no time frame for 'going pro'. Everyone is different, so just use your judgement.

I

SEEING
SIGNS

DEVELOPING
YOUR PSYCHIC
ABILITIES

Diviners are often thought of as 'readers'. Card-slingers read the Tarot. Scryers read crystal balls. Dream interpreters read the symbols that appear during our sleep. However, while it is true that all diviners are readers, not all readers are diviners. There is a significant difference. A reader is someone who can read the messages presented by a particular form of divination. Readers know that crows are associated with death, for instance, or that the Magician Tarot card predicts new opportunities. A reader merely 'reads' what they see based on their understanding of a symbol.

A diviner is someone who also knows that crows symbolize death and that the Magician Tarot card can predict new opportunities. But the diviner's divination is not just reserved for the reading table: diviners feel a strong spiritual connection to a higher being, the universe and the spirits. Diviners are in constant contact with the divine. A reader performs a reading, but being a diviner is a way of life.

For the diviner, set readings with Tarot cards and crystal balls are merely one facet of their divination. They understand that the power of divination is a constant presence, and they can receive signs and messages from the spirits at every turn. Learning to be more in touch with the spiritual world and becoming a diviner will enhance your psychic development, which, in turn, will improve the accuracy of your readings.

It is much better to be a diviner than a reader, because a diviner develops and uses their awareness of being continuously surrounded by the spirit world. Diviners receive constant confirmation that their ancestors and passed loved ones are around them, helping them to form their interpretations, which in turn lends conviction to their readings.

Doubting your readings is a significant roadblock to confidently practising divination. When you first become a reader, you will constantly be plagued by doubt. You will question whether you're reading the 'right' way, whether your reading makes sense and whether your predictions are true. Doubt and lack of belief are the main reasons why most newbie readers abandon their divination practice.

If you evolve from being a reader to a diviner, you will eliminate any doubt you have over the accuracy of your readings, because you will forever be receiving confirmation that the spirit is around you and assisting you, not just with your readings but with your life choices in general.

By being a diviner, you will also learn to trust the universe and believe in divine planning. Even if you don't get favourable results during divination, you will rarely view a reading as negative because you are safe in the knowledge that everything is eventually going to work out: a failed relationship is merely an opportunity to meet someone better; the loss of a job is the universe clearing a person's path towards their true calling.

When you start to practise divination you will be a reader, but a diviner is what you should aim to become. To become a diviner you must observe the signs the spirits send you. As we touched on in the Introduction, following signs, or apantomancy, is a method of divination in itself. For example, the belief that finding four-leaf clovers or pennies is lucky also counts as apantomancy. However, messages from spirits can be anything that is spiritually significant to you.

WHY DO SPIRITS SEND SIGNS?

You're probably wondering why spirits would send you signs and not just appear to you in full form. Why would they bother sending you feathers or rainbows when they could easily manifest as fully formed people?

Many people, even readers who practise divination, are afraid of spirits. Most people have been conditioned to believe that spirits are entities that can possess them, control their minds and drag their souls to hell. Even the spirit of your beloved auntie would strike fear if she caught you off guard in the middle of the night in a dimly lit kitchen!

To counteract your fear, spirits will instead begin by opening up to you slowly. They will test the waters of communication with signs. In a way, connecting with spirits is like connecting with someone you have romantic feelings for; you will casually like each other's posts on social media before you jump feet first into direct messaging – and with the spirits, it's no different.

To work with spirits, you have to let them know that communicating with you is OK. By being mindful of the signs they send you, you're telling them that they are not overstepping the mark by reaching out to you in this way.

A spirit will start by sending you physical signs, but their connection to you will grow and strengthen. You'll begin to receive messages from the spirits in your dreams, and they will work with you during your readings by inspiring images and messages in your third eye (the place where you receive psychic information).

This is one of the reasons why becoming a diviner (and not just a reader) will make your readings clearer and more accurate. Giving spirits permission to communicate with you through signs will further open up the channels of communication between you when you are reading. To start with, you may receive only the odd sign here and there, but eventually you will feel the influence of the spirits when you work with the Tarot, crystals, tea leaves, dreams, palmistry and all other kinds of divination.

THE PURPOSE OF SIGNS

To begin with, spirits will send you signs just so that they can communicate to you that they are around. But, as time goes on, they will start to send you signs as a way to help you overcome major life dilemmas.

For example, when I first became a professional reader, I really struggled with the fact that I did not know if I was doing the right thing. I knew that starting a business was a massive financial and emotional risk. At that time I had no money, no professional contacts and nothing to help me springboard my career; all I had was a passion for divination.

I

As soon as I started my business, I began to see rainbows everywhere. I was seeing them so often, I started to photograph and document them. Not only would I catch sight of actual physical rainbows, but I would often see the pattern of a rainbow, hear the word 'rainbow' or see reflections appear as rainbows.

These rainbows seemed to appear during times of stress. They would pop up whenever I needed reassurance, and surface just before I had a reading to perform. I started to realize that these rainbows were messages from the spirits, which provided 'proof' that I was divinely supported. I continued with my career in divination and I now teach fortune-telling full-time.

WHO WILL SEND YOU SIGNS?

There is not one specific spirit that sends everyone everywhere signs; you will have different guiding spirits from your friends. Signs are often sent by one soul or a group of souls. These spirits will be the souls of people who have a vested interest in your success and who want you to do well.

It is most common for the spirits of passed loved ones or the spirits of ancestors to send us signs. Because they are the spirits of relatives, they want to watch you be happy and make good decisions. Even if you have never met your ancestors in real life, or cannot remember doing so, they are still likely to be your spirit guides and attempt to communicate with you. If there is someone you're extremely close to who has passed, that individual will usually be the person who sends you signs and messages. Or the first person in spirit who pops into your head might be the one who contacts you; because they are at the forefront of your mind, they are near to you spiritually.

WHICH SIGNS?

As we have seen, there are some things that people automatically associate with spirits, such as white feathers, rainbows and ladybirds, but these aren't the only signs you can receive. A sign from a spirit can take any form, but for it to qualify as a true sign it must be something that is either significant to you, or to your ancestors, or something that you may see often but which has special associations for you.

I associate bees with my grandad's spirit, because before he died he allowed me to hold them in my hand so that I wouldn't be afraid of them. Now, whenever he sends me signs, they always appear in the form of a bee because these insects are significant in our relationship. Your signs from your ancestral spirits will differ from mine. You may, for instance, see the scarab beetle as a sign because your ancestors were Egyptian; scarabs were sacred to Egyptians because their movements were thought to symbolize the daily journey of the sun. Or you may have noticed that you see depictions of roses over and over again, so that could be your sign. What qualifies as a sign for one person will not be a sign for someone else.

INTERPRETING YOUR SIGNS

A sign is very different from a symbol. Signs are reassuring and comforting, whereas symbols can be considered either positive or negative depending on their history and associations.

The meaning of a sign is not the same as the meaning of a

symbol. For example, apples are often symbolically associated with sexuality, temptation and magic. Christian art often depicts the apple as the fruit of temptation, and they feature in fairy tales such as 'Snow White'. In many ways, apples have a sinister symbolic interpretation. However, you may view apples differently because your favourite aunt used to own an apple farm. For you, seeing real apples and paintings of apples, hearing the word 'apple' and smelling the scent of apples might be positive omens and signs that bring you peace of mind.

While symbols can have many and contrasting connotations, signs are usually always affirmative. If you're struggling to decide whether or not to do something, signs are messages from the spirits showing you that you should follow your heart and desires. Signs are your ancestors' way of telling you that all will work out for the best.

IS THIS REALLY A SIGN?

When you first begin to practise divination, you will question your interpretations, and you may struggle with whether or not a sign is really a sign or just a figment of your imagination. Working with signs and developing a bond with the spirits will help eliminate your doubts over the accuracy of your readings. This is why, especially at the beginning, I recommend that you always ask the spirit for confirmation. To do this, simply ask to see the sign again.

In some cultures, people are taught that asking God or spirits for divine confirmation is blasphemous. However, from a spiritual standpoint, there is nothing wrong with asking spirits for confirmation, especially if you are not sure whether something is a true message or sign. In fact, a little natural scepticism when you're working with spirits is a good thing, because it will keep you grounded.

HOW TO WORK WITH SIGNS

Now we are going to look at how you can start your journey as a diviner and begin to receive signs from the spirits.

WHO IS SENDING YOU SIGNS?

The first step is to identify of the main spirit who sends you signs. While you may have several spirits sending you signs at any given time, there will be one in particular who is at the head of your spiritual army. As mentioned earlier, they may be a passed relative who randomly pops into your head because they will already be close to you on a spiritual level.

However, sometimes we can have spirits who are close to us whom we have never met in real life or cannot remember meeting. If this relates to you, do not worry! You can still form a healthy relationship with this spirit, and they will assist you during your divination journey.

ASSIGN A SIGN

Establishing whether you know the spirit personally will affect the type of sign you receive. If you had a relationship with the spirit in life, they will send you signs that will be significant to your relationship. For example, if you associate lilies with Granny, she will send you signs in the form of lilies.

If you have never had a relationship with your main spirit, they will send you signs that are either culturally significant to you, or something that you are likely to keep noticing. I knew my great-grandmother, but could not remember her well, so when I became a professional diviner she began to send me rainbows, because this was something I was likely to pay attention to.

If you do not know what your sign is likely to be, you can pick something you like or feel drawn to. Your sign can be an animal, a shape, a flower, a mineral, etc. There are no hard and fast rules.

It is a good idea to establish your sign before you start to look for it. Set the intention that you are going to view that sign as a message from the spirits. Once you have established your sign, you can start to ask for it.

ASK FOR YOUR SIGN

You can ask the spirits around you for your sign right now. Even just thinking about how you would like to receive your sign is good enough for your spirits. The spirits of your ancestors do not need an elaborate ritual to get the ball rolling. Once you put out the intention that you would like to start receiving signs, you will.

RECEIVING SIGNS

As you go about your life, be mindful that you are likely to observe your sign in some form throughout the day. You may even find that you see your sign in a variety of ways. Let's take the lily as an example. You may see real lily flowers, catch a glimpse of lilies in a wallpaper pattern or hear the name 'Lily'.

ASK FOR CONFIRMATION
OF YOUR SIGN

If you receive your sign but doubt has naturally entered your mind, don't worry! You will receive confirmation. Soon enough, you will receive as many signs as you need to dispel any scepticism you have about the presence of your spirits.

Once you receive your sign, congratulations! You are now a diviner forming a close relationship with the spirits for the purpose of improving your psychic readings and spiritual development.

Next, we are going to look at another way in which you can strengthen your psychic awareness by improving your intuition with the help of one of the most famous divination tools on the planet – the crystal ball.

II

CRYSTAL
BALL
SCRYING

FOR CONNECTING
TO YOUR
INTUITION

W hile apantomancy will lead you to strengthen your psychic capabilities by developing your relationship with the external spirit world, there are other divination methods you can use to grow your psychic abilities from the inside.

Your ancestors will always be around you and will always send you signs. When you're divining, they will constantly be communicating and working with you. However, although you should continue to deepen your relationship with your spirits, you should also aim to strengthen your own intuitive abilities. Developing a strong intuition ensures that when your ancestors speak, you'll hear them.

Your intuition is your sixth sense. It's the sense you use to receive direct messages from your spirits. There are many ways in which you can develop your intuition, but the use of crystals is one of the most popular and accessible. Crystals have long been associated with divination; in fact, the ancient Mayans divined using obsidian (volcanic glass), which they shaped into flawless mirrors. In modern times you can buy not only mirrors but also crystal balls, pendulums, runes and thumbed stones, which can all be used for prediction. You can buy crystals in the form of geodes or carved into spheres, wands and even animals of every species and colour. Your love of divination will introduce you to all things crystals. The opposite is also true: lots of people discover divination through their love of crystal healing.

In this book, we are going to cover a range of divination methods that require the use of crystals. First, we will look at one of the most famous fortune-telling tools: the crystal ball. Most people associate divination with crystal spheres. While the old Gypsy fortune-teller sitting in a darkened room with her glowing crystal ball can be seen as a cliché, there is some truth to the myths surrounding crystal ball divination, also known as scrying.

Crystal balls can indeed be used for divination, but they are often not used in the way you might expect. The vast majority of diviners do not see pictures or symbols in their crystal balls. Instead, most scryers use their crystal balls as meditative tools to help them access and strengthen their intuition. To use a crystal ball properly, you must first understand what intuition is, and where it comes from.

WHAT IS INTUITION?

Intuition is that strange feeling in your gut or niggle in the back of your mind that tells you whether or not something is a good idea. Typically, intuition requires no outside information or input.

For example, as you're driving your car, you get a hunch. Instead of driving straight down the motorway as you usually would, you get a feeling that you should take the exit instead. Later, you discover there were roadworks, that would have held you up in traffic for hours. You avoided the congestion thanks to your intuition.

WHERE DOES INTUITION COME FROM?

Everyone has a soul. Most people think of it as a ball of energy contained within the body. Although I know the soul to exist and believe that everyone has a soul, I do not agree that it lives entirely within the physical body. Only a small aspect of your soul can be found in your body; the majority of it exists in the spirit world with other souls and spirits.

You are always in communication with your spirit-self, the part of your soul that exists in the spirit world. Because the spirit-self is part of you, you are always connected and will forever be linked to your spirit. When your physical body dies, you will return to your spirit-self in the spirit world.

Because the spirit-self is in the spirit realm, it knows all and sees all – past, present and future. Your intuition – those gut feelings – is essentially formed by you receiving information from your spirit-self. Unless you have a strong sense of intuition, you might not always hear your spirit-self, but this does not mean it isn't relaying information to you. So how can you develop your intuition and create a better connection with your spirit-self?

YOU ARE INTUITIVE

Many people believe that they have to display psychic abilities from a young age to be talented in this area. They worry that they cannot practise divination because they are not 'psychic' enough. This is especially true for those people who have taken up the interest in spirituality late in life. However, even if you don't realize it, you are a natural intuitive.

For whatever reason, some people are born with a naturally strong connection to their spirit-self. Some can 'hear' their spirit more clearly, and these people are what most of us would deem 'intuitive'. But, in reality, everyone is connected to their spirit-self, so everyone is intuitive, whether you hear your spirit-self loud and clear or whether it's more of a faint whisper. For those who struggle, the good news is that intuition can always be worked on. You may think of it as a 'gift' that only some people have, but, as we have seen, this is not true. Everyone, including you, is naturally intuitive and connected to their spirit-self. So everyone, especially you, can access and strengthen their intuition.

DIVINERS NEED THEIR INTUITION

You access your intuition all the time without realizing it. You cannot start a new relationship, run a business, raise kids or even drive a car without the input of your spirit-self. The ways in which you receive this input, however, may not be obvious to you.

You must have a clear mind to be able to access your intuition. If you have too much mental noise, you will not be able to hear your spirit-self clearly; you will struggle to tap in to your intuition and may miss its insights.

To develop your intuition, you need to partake in activities that quiet mental chatter. Otherwise, your intuition may talk to you very directly, but it will be mixed in with your own thoughts. If you want to perform true readings, you must be able to drown out your conscious thoughts and tune in to your intuition; otherwise, you're not really performing a reading – you're just picking cards or throwing runes and giving advice based on the thoughts in your head rather than the messages you receive from the spirit world.

Your intuition may feel like an uncontrollable beast that you cannot tame. Your ability to receive messages will seem to be all over the place. Do not worry, because – with the right tools and techniques – you can gain control.

ACCESSING YOUR INTUITION

When trying to solve a problem or discover the answers to a question, many people get their best breakthroughs when they are exercising or taking a shower. During a brisk walk, for instance, what was once an impassable mental mountain suddenly seems like a molehill. The reason for this is that simple activities can help clear the mind. The clearer your conscious mind is, the louder you can hear your spirit-self.

Meditation is one avenue towards a clearer mind. However, in many ways meditation is not always practical for a diviner – and this is especially true if your seeker is already sitting in front of you, waiting for their reading. If you get out of the zone, they may view it as inappropriate if you stop the reading so that you can meditate. Therefore, you may need a tool that can put you in a meditative state without meaning you have to break away from your seeker. One of those tools is a crystal ball.

Staring into a crystal sphere offers a route to meditation that does not require you to be in silence or in solitude, focusing on your own thoughts. The shape of a sphere and its reflections of patterns and colours are entrancing. It is very easy to get lost inside a crystal ball. As you stare into your crystal, everything will become clearer to you. Your conscious mind will quieten and your intuitive voice will sing. Even better, it is not hard to get started with a crystal ball – you can stare into your sphere and begin the meditative process in seconds.

HOW TO WORK WITH A CRYSTAL BALL

SELECT YOUR SPHERE

Contrary to popular belief, not all crystal balls are made from true crystals. In fact, most are actually glass, because glass is a lot less expensive and more accessible than quartz crystal.

Most diviners start their crystal ball journey with glass spheres. To be honest, there is no reason why you should not choose a glass ball over a crystal one, as they both work the same way – and either will help you to access your intuition.

Once you get the hang of using a sphere, you can decide whether you want to invest in a ball made from real quartz crystal.

SELECT YOUR SIZE

Once you decide whether you're going to buy a sphere made from glass or crystal, you must choose the right size.

Most spheres are between 50 and 70 mm in diameter. I believe that this is the ideal size for a sphere – any less than 50 mm and your sphere will be difficult to use. You may be tempted to purchase an extremely large sphere, but I feel that a sphere that is bigger than 90 mm in diameter is also a challenge. If your ball is too small or too big, its size can distract you, so try to stay within the ideal range of 50 to 70 mm.

You can purchase a sphere online or from your local mind, body, spirit shop. The product description should state its size. Most spheres come with a stand that will be the right size for its circumference.

USE YOUR SPHERE

Once you have your sphere and its stand, you can begin practising. It is a good idea to start using your divination objects straight away, because the only way in which you can connect to them is by using them. There does not have to be a grace period between purchasing a divination object and using one – you're born ready!

To use your sphere, place it on a flat surface and make sure that it is steady and not moving. Stare into your sphere and get lost in its brilliance.

PETITION YOUR ANCESTORS

By now, if you have begun to work with signs (see Chapter 1), you have probably received a sign or two from your ancestors during your day-to-day life. These signs will help to reassure you that spirits are always around you. Evidence of spirits will, in turn, build your confidence in your readings.

Although your intention for this starter reading is to receive messages from your intuition, you can ask your ancestors to help you achieve this goal. Your ancestral spirits can help you to hear your spirit-self more clearly whether you're reading for yourself or for other people. Either in your head or out loud, ask them if they will assist you in deciphering messages from your intuition, and in performing the best crystal ball reading possible.

RECEIVE MESSAGES

As you stare into your sphere, try to calm your mind. If there is something that you are heavily preoccupied by and worrying about, acknowledge these feelings, but do not dwell on them – instead, bring your focus and energy to watching the sphere.

While observing the sphere, you will notice your inner voice begin to talk to you. You may brush this off as thoughts, but they are not regular thoughts – this is your intuition (or spirit-self) speaking to you. We will cover how to distinguish between your intuition and your conscious thoughts in the next chapter, but for now, know that staring into a crystal ball will cause your inner voice to become more apparent to you.

WRITE IT DOWN

Once you've finished staring into your crystal ball, you can record your thoughts in a journal or special diary that you assign for the purpose of recording the results of your divination. It is a good idea to write down what you've picked up on during divination, so that you can refer to this information later.

Some of the impressions you have obtained from your crystal sphere may not make sense to you just yet, whereas others will very clearly be relevant to your life right now. Diviners always write down everything because this is a good way to measure the accuracy of your readings.

While the crystal ball can be used to strengthen and help you understand your intuitive voice, there are other methods of divination you can practise that will help you to get more direct answers and information. Next, we will look at a super-simple way in which you can get definitive answers to your most burning questions.

III

—

PENDULUM DOWSING

—

FOR ANSWERING EVERYDAY 'YES OR NO' QUESTIONS

Most would-be diviners are attracted to divination because they like the thought of having their questions answered. One of the reasons I have stuck so religiously to my diviner lifestyle is that I enjoy the fact that I can use my divination to determine the outcome of an event, help make better choices or predict the future of a relationship.

The simple methods of divination we have looked at so far will give you answers and help you to predict events. However, it is natural to lack confidence in these methods when you start out. For example, you have to practise apantomancy for a while before you develop 100 per cent faith that the signs you're receiving come from your ancestors and not just your imagination. Similarly, you have to perform many crystal ball readings before you stop second-guessing whether or not your predictions are coming from your intuition.

If you have had the opportunity to practise apantomancy or crystal ball reading, the chances are that you performed these readings for yourself. In a way, it can be more challenging to read for yourself than for other people because you are more emotionally invested in the situation. Having a lot riding on the matter can cause you to question the accuracy of your divination.

There are a couple of ways in which you can learn how to distinguish between messages from your spirit-self and those of your conscious thoughts and feelings. This will help you gain confidence in your readings.

DISTINGUISHING BETWEEN
EMOTION AND INTUITION

Although emotions are good for us, they can hold us back from trusting our divination. When the emotional stakes in a reading are high, you can start to second-guess whether your reading is accurate, because your instincts are to avoid anything that might cause you physical or emotional pain.

This is true for readings that appear to have either extremely negative or positive predictions. If the reading has a negative outcome, you might dismiss it because you do not want the future to play out the way you predicted. On the other hand, if your reading looks too good to be true, your instinct may be to brush it off as inaccurate, because you want to avoid the possibility of disappointment. So, as a diviner, your job is to build trust in yourself and your divination.

Completely eradicating emotion is not possible. It is natural to experience some level of fear, doubt or insecurity, and for these emotions to affect your readings. Your natural human fear will shut you down or put you in denial. However, there are ways in which you can separate your intuitive voice from your fears.

Your intuition is very matter-of-fact because it does not have an ego that can be crushed by a certain outcome. Instead of going into a panic because your divination has predicted that you're not going to get the outcome you wanted, your intuitive voice will give you other options.

Let's look at an example. Shona has applied for her dream position and asks, 'Will I get this job?' She then performs a reading that tells her she will not get the position. How does she know that this is accurate?

Her fear will tell her that her dreams are over. According to her fear, her life is terrible and there is nothing she can do about it. She may even not believe the reading.

If it was her intuition talking, however, Shona would see other options. Although she may be upset that she will not get the position she wants, her intuition will say, 'Hey, this isn't going to work out; it isn't the right job for you after all, but you can always try this instead...' Intuitive information is pro-active.

GROWING USED TO THE SOUND
OF YOUR INTUITIVE VOICE

The intuitive voice is high-spirited without being naïve. While your spirit-self can acknowledge that you will not receive the outcome you desire, it will not make you feel as though there is nothing you can do about your current situation.

As a diviner, you must exercise your ability to hear your intuitive voice. While we have previously learned how to use a crystal ball and looked at strengthening our intuitive voice, we can also develop our connection with that voice by making simple predictions and answering simple, specific questions using a dowsing pendulum.

Practising this way will allow you to distinguish between your thoughts and your intuition, and set you up for the methods of divination that you'll discover in the coming chapters.

DISCOVER YOUR DEFAULT REACTION

In order to learn the difference between your conscious voice and your intuitive voice, you need to acknowledge your default reaction to divination. Your default reaction will depend on whether you are a positive or a negative thinker.

A negative thinker will see the bad in everything, to the extent that it clouds their judgement. If you're a negative thinker, and you have received a 'yes' in your reading, you will not believe the reading because you will not want to get your hopes up. When negative thinkers receive a 'no' in their readings, they take it as evidence of their suspicions.

When positive thinkers get a 'yes', they simply gather up their cards or crystals and go about their lives. If positive thinkers get a 'no' in their readings, their first reaction is to ignore the reading because they are in denial.

Everyone will fall into one of the above camps, and you are no exception, but you might not be consistently positive or consistently negative. You might be a positive thinker when it comes to your friendships, but a negative thinker in your romantic relationships or when it comes to your work, or vice versa.

Your job as a diviner is to distinguish between your default emotional reaction and your intuition, but you must first know what your default reaction sounds like. What is your first instinct? You're going to find out with the help of dowsing.

DOWSING

Dowsing is any method of divination that uses a swaying object to predict an outcome. In modern times, the most popular type of dowsing involves crystals, but dowsing rods were common in the twentieth century and rings tied to string were all the rage back in the Middle Ages.

Unlike other divination techniques, dowsing will not bombard you with information – instead, you will receive a simple 'yes' or 'no' answer. This will allow you to become aware of your default reaction: is your instinct to be overly optimistic or extremely negative?

When your pendulum gives you a 'yes' or 'no', you will hear the sound of your conscious thoughts instantly either agreeing or disagreeing with the outcome. With practice, you will get to know what your conscious thoughts sound like, and you will learn how your journey into self-doubt plays out. Recognizing your emotions when they pop up will help you to work out how they try to influence your readings.

LISTENING TO YOUR INTUITION

Of course, the goal of the following exercise is not to use your conscious instincts to answer questions. The goal is to give you the tools to expose your doubts and your natural inclinations so that you can push past them and give accurate readings using your intuition alone.

You can discover the 'voice' of your intuition by going beyond your default emotional reaction. When your default reaction enters your mind, imagine asking your spirit-self, 'That is fine, but how can I improve on this?' Or, 'What can I do to make this better?' You will then hear your intuition provide you with options.

HOW TO ANSWER A QUESTION USING A PENDULUM

———

PICK YOUR PENDULUM

There is a wide range of pendulums on the market, and some are very inexpensive, made from wood or brass. Although there are more cost-effective ways to obtain your pendulum, I believe that it is best to purchase one made from real crystal.

Because we are using the pendulum for an intuitive exercise, it is a very good idea to select a crystal that is associated with psychic development. You can learn more about crystal associations in Chapter 6, but as a general rule, clear, blue and purple crystals increase intuition. Therefore, it is best to purchase a pendulum that is made from clear quartz, amethyst or lapis lazuli, for example.

MAKE A LIST OF QUESTIONS YOU
WOULD LIKE ANSWERED

Write down your questions before you begin your divination. As for scrying, you might like to keep a journal specifically for this purpose. By recording your questions you can avoid any doubt about what you're actually asking, or the accuracy of the answers.

PETITION YOUR ANCESTORS

As with every reading, you should ask your ancestors to help you perform your reading to the best of your ability. Set the intention that you would like an accurate answer to whichever question you have recorded in your journal.

ASK YOUR PENDULUM A QUESTION

To perform a pendulum reading, hold the chain of the pendulum between your thumb and forefinger. The hand you choose to hold your pendulum with is a personal choice and does not make any difference to the accuracy of your reading.

While holding the pendulum, ask it one of the questions on your list. Be sure to read out your question exactly as it is written down in your journal. Your pendulum will naturally sway. Try not to influence the movement of the pendulum; keep your hand as still as you possibly can, and allow the pendulum to move as it wills.

If the pendulum moves to the right, this means 'yes'. If your pendulum swings to the left, this means 'no'. Backward and forward motions are not as common, but if this happens the answer is 'maybe' or 'possibly, but not right now'.

TAKE NOTE OF YOUR DEFAULT REACTION

When you receive your 'yes' or 'no', what are your first thoughts? Is your initial reaction to say, 'Oh, well, that's great'? Or is your first instinct to think, 'I knew it, my life is over'? Remember, neither one is good or bad; you're only trying to register (and remember!) what your conscious voice sounds like so that you can distinguish it from your intuition.

GET BEYOND YOUR DEFAULT REACTION

Having a default reaction is perfectly normal – everyone has one. However, if you want to practise divination, you must push your instincts to one side and ask your spirit-self, 'OK, that is how I feel – but what should I do?'

Because you are part of your spirit-self, your intuitive voice will naturally be within you; it probably sounds a lot like your own voice. However, instead of being emotional, super-depressing or insanely optimistic, your intuition will be very matter-of-fact. It will give you options for how to proceed, and say things such as: 'That's not going to work out, but we could always try x.' Or 'Maybe I should do x instead.'

If your reading does not include one form of advice or another, you are working entirely from your conscious mind and default reactions. Intuitive readings will always give you options!

While dowsing offers simple yet direct answers, if you wish to develop your divination skills, it's valuable to explore more complicated systems. This is why we are going to explore how to read the Lenormand oracle next.

IV

—

READING
LENORMAND
CARDS

—

FOR PREDICTING
YOUR GENERAL
FORTUNE

hile getting 'yes' or 'no' answers is always fun in dowsing, the real beauty of divination comes from predicting the future of your life. As diviners, we differentiate between a specific reading (a reading that answers a specific question or focuses on a particular life area) and a general reading (a reading that reveals your general fortune with no particular agenda).

Performing general readings with divination tools such as cards can be a little more challenging than answering 'yes' or 'no' with a pendulum. With a pendulum reading, you can only receive a 'yes', 'no' or 'maybe'. In general readings, there are infinite possibilities as to what can be divined. This is why to practise divination, you need:

- a strong connection to your ancestors;

- good intuition;

- the ability to tell the difference between emotion and intuition.

You are now going to take everything you have learned so far and predict your general fortune using Lenormand cards.

Lenormand cards were invented in Europe about 200 years ago. The structure and symbolism of the Lenormand system is based on tea leaf reading. The cards are named after Emperor Napoleon's fortune-teller, Madame Lenormand (1772–1843), but she did not create them; following her death, they were named in her honour.

A Lenormand deck consists of 36 cards that depict items from everyday life. Each one of these items has its own symbolic meaning. The great thing about Lenormand cards is that once you've learned the meanings of the symbols, you can apply them in other methods of divination. For example, in Lenormand readings, the Scythe card represents accidents or endings. If you dream about a scythe or see one in a crystal ball, this symbol has the same meaning. As you live your diviner lifestyle, you will realize that all methods of divination share similarities. For example, the character on the Death Tarot card holds a scythe: again, this card predicts the ending of a relationship or situation. Things that you learn in one mode of fortune-telling can be applied to another. Learning how to use one tool makes it easier to use another.

LENORMAND CARD MEANINGS

Here is a list of the Lenormand cards and what they represent:

1. RIDER: NEWS
messages, visitors,
messengers, acts.

2. LOVER: LUCK
fun, chance, games, jokes,
coincidence, serendipity.

3. HIP: TRAVEL
movement, adventure,
holidays, mode
of transportation.

4. HOME: HOME
comfort, safety, immediate
surroundings, close family.

5. TREE:
EXTENDED FAMILY
genetics, DNA, health,
oxygen, forests.

6. CLOUDS: CONFUSION
uncertainty, negative
thinkers, dark thoughts,
the weather.

7. SNAKE: JEALOUSY
false friends, envy, infidelity,
competitors, reptiles.

8. COFFIN: DEATH
serious illness, endings,
people from the past,
situations fading away.

9. BOUQUET: GIFTS
values, morals, ethics, beauty,
decorations, surprises.

10. SCYTHE: ACCIDENTS
shocks, situations being
quickly cut out of your life,
warnings.

11. WHIP: ABUSE
arguments, strife, things that
happen repeatedly, sports.

12. BIRDS: CHATTER
gossip, social media,
communication in real time,
birds, twins.

13. CHILD: CHILDREN
small things, little, tiny,
childish, playful, innocence.

14. FOX:
ENTREPRENEURSHIP
jobs, careers, con-artists,
creativity, cunning, slyness.

15. BEAR:
AUTHORITY FIGURES
mothers, bosses, weight,
lifestyle, strength, power, force.

16. STARS: WISHES
celebrity, hope, progress,
positive thinkers, inspiration.

17. STORK: PREGNANCY
babies, change, meta-
morphosis, relocation,
emigration.

18. DOG: FRIENDS
confidants, followers, trust,
loyalty, pets.

19. TOWER:
THE GOVERNMENT
official, associations,
buildings, standing out.

20. GARDEN:
WIDER SOCIAL CIRCLE
society, parties, gatherings,
important dates.

21. MOUNTAIN: LONG-
TERM SITUATIONS
years, problems, road-blocks,
impassable obstacles,
literal mountains.

22. CROSSROADS:
CHOICES
dilemmas, multiple options,
alternative roads, an
alternative person.

23. MICE: STRESS
anxiety, contagious illnesses,
theft, situations that are
eating away at you.

24. HEART: LOVE
relationships, romance,
priorities, feelings, where
your heart lies, the physical
heart.

25. RING: COMMITMENT
contracts, bindings both
legal and emotional,
engagements, jewellery.

26. BOOK: SECRETS
knowledge, education,
learning, experts,
discoveries, books.

27. LETTER: LETTERS
paper, invoices, certificates,
forms, packages, emails,
direct messages.

28. MAN: YOU
(if you are male)
OR YOUR LOVER
(if you are female).

29. WOMAN: YOU
(if you are female)
OR YOUR LOVER
(if you are male). (See below
for notes on reading for
same-sex relationships.)

30. LILY: PEACE
calm, contentment,
old age, experience,
retirement, sex, sexuality.

31. SUN: SUCCESS
triumph, accomplishment,
happiness, heat,
warm place.

32. MOON: INTUITION
magic, psychic ability,
reputation, spotlight,
recognition, cycles.

**33. KEY: IMPORTANT
MATTERS**
serious, urgent, needs
dealing with now, safes,
locks, keys.

34. FISH: MONEY
financial, business, trades,
assets, stocks and shares,
flow, water.

35. ANCHOR: STABILITY
stuck, consistent features
or people in your life,
the beach.

36. CROSS: BURDEN
struggle, pain, sacrifice,
symbolism, religion,
fate, destiny.

In the Lenormand, the Man or Woman card represents the seeker (depending on their gender). The remaining card symbolizes the seeker's lover. So, if you are female the Woman card represents you, and the Man is your partner (or future partner). However, most modern Lenormand decks include an extra Man and Woman card so that those who don't identify as heterosexual can swap out the Man or Woman cards as they choose. For example, a lesbian may include two Woman cards instead of a Man and Woman card in their deck. Just be sure to decide which card represents the seeker and which is their partner before you start the reading, as not having these in place early on can cause confusion.

Lenormand cards are always read in combination with each other, or in combination with their position in the spread (see more on spreads below). So, if I want to predict what is going to happen in my day, I will pull a string of two or more cards from the top of a shuffled deck, and combine their individual meanings to form one overall meaning. For example:

CLOVER & BIRDS
today, I will have fun on social media.

WOMAN & MOON
today, I will get to exercise my intuition.

LILY & HEART & MAN
today, I will find peace and love with my partner.

Although you can pull 'strings' of cards in Lenormand to determine your fortune in the short term, it's best if you use Lenormand for more general readings that cover longer periods. You can do this by performing a Grand Tableau spread.

THE GRAND TABLEAU SPREAD

In divination, it is customary to use 'spreads'. A spread is the position that the cards are laid out in, and there are many types. Each position in the spread has a set meaning. One position in the spread may represent the past, one could represent the positives, while another could represent the action you should take, and so on. In a spread, the interpretation of each card is influenced by its own inherent meaning combined with the meaning of its position in the spread.

In the Lenormand, the most popular spread is the Grand Tableau. This has 36 positions, which cover every area of life, from love, career and business to social media – even letters you might receive or books you might have read. Opposite is an example of a Grand Tableau spread with its positions numbered. You're probably thinking, 'Wow, I don't want to memorize 36 spread positions!' Do not worry, each position's meaning corresponds to a card's number (see the list of the Lenormand card meanings above). The first position is known as the House of Rider, and it represents news you're going to receive. The second position is called the House of Clover and predicts your future luck. The twenty-fifth house is called the House of Ring and will reveal your commitments, and so on.

When you're reading a Grand Tableau spread, you can interpret every single house, or you can use your intuition to read only those houses that you feel drawn to – whether that be only one house, five houses or a range of positions. If you're reading intuitively, the positions that contain the most important information will grab your attention and draw you to them.

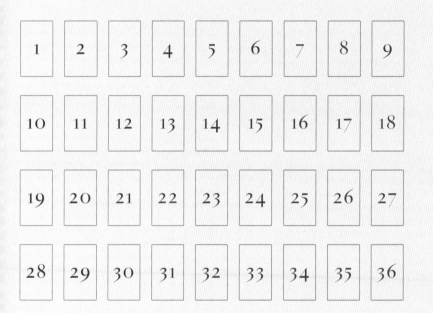

The house positions in the Lenormand Grand Tableau spread.

HOW TO PERFORM A LENORMAND READING

SOURCING YOUR LENORMAND CARDS

The Lenormand system has only recently seen a surge in popularity, but you may be lucky enough to find a deck in your local mind, body, spirit shop or bookshop. If you have difficulty finding a deck locally, you can easily purchase one online.

ASK FOR ANCESTRAL ASSISTANCE

As with all methods of divination, when performing a Lenormand reading, it is good practice always to ask your ancestral spirits to help you perform the reading. I always say, 'Dear ancestors, help me to perform the best and most accurate reading possible for everyone involved.' You can design your own petition prayer or use mine.

SET A TIME FRAME

It is easy enough to predict that you will lose your job, but what good is this information if you do not know when it will happen? Everyone can naturally see into the future, but some people can predict events in a few weeks' time, while others can see years ahead. Just as you have default emotional reactions, you also have a default reading time.

You will not know how far ahead your default time frame is until you have measured your readings. But you probably don't want to wait months or years before you can work out how long on average your readings take to play out. So, to counteract this it's best to set a time frame, especially in general readings where you aren't searching for answers to specific questions.

Once I have asked my ancestors for their help, I set my time frame. For the sake of this exercise, let's say that we are reading for Kate, who wishes to know what is coming up in her short-term future. I ask my cards, 'What is going to happen for Kate in the next three months?'

I recommend that you likewise read for three months, six months or a year into the future, depending on your needs.

SHUFFLE YOUR CARDS

For card readings, you can shuffle your deck as you would a deck of playing cards. The first time you shuffle your cards you'll need to shuffle them for a long time to get them out of order. In the future, you will not have to shuffle them as much.

While shuffling, think of your intention for the reading. In this case, we are asking, 'What is going to happen for Kate in the next three months?' It is perfectly OK if your mind begins to wander –

you can acknowledge your thoughts, but try to bring them back to your question. Some mind wandering cannot be helped. What matters most is that you begin your reading with the set intention of predicting your (or someone else's) future.

Some readers like to shuffle their cards a set number of times, but I recommend that you only shuffle until you intuitively feel ready to stop. When it is time to stop shuffling, your spirit-self will tell you. You will hear your inner voice say, 'That's enough.'

LAY OUT YOUR CARDS

For the Grand Tableau spread, you will use your entire Lenormand deck. There are different methods of laying out the cards for this spread, but the most popular method (and the one I recommend) takes the shape of four rows of nine cards. Lay your cards out one by one from left to right. Lay down position 1 first, then position 2, and so on (see diagram on page 63).

You can turn your cards over as you lay them out, or place them all face down and turn them over when they are all in position. Everyone has their preference and does things differently. To be honest, it makes little difference when you turn them over; all that matters is the accuracy of your reading.

INTERPRET YOUR READING

I have set the intention for Kate's reading and laid out her cards. I am not going to interpret every single position in the spread; I am just going to read the houses that I feel intuitively drawn to. In Kate's case, I feel particularly interested in the following houses:

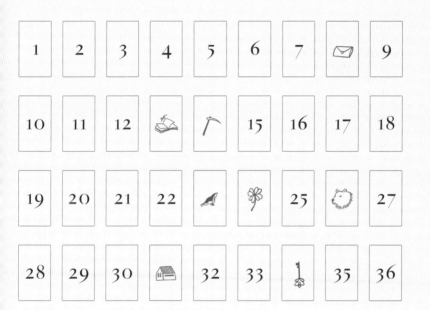

The chosen cards and their houses in Kate's Grand Tableau spread.

Here is how I would interpret Kate's reading, based on the cards' meanings, the houses they have landed in and my intuition:

8. THE HOUSE OF COFFIN
in the Coffin House, Kate has the Letter card. Intuitively, I feel that this means she is going to receive a message from a person in her past.

13. THE HOUSE OF CHILD
the Book in the House of Child means that a younger person in Kate's life will soon enter education.

14. THE HOUSE OF FOX
Kate has the Scythe in the House of Fox – the career position. She should be cautious of her surroundings as this combination can predict an accident at work.

23. THE HOUSE OF MICE
the House of Mice represents the stresses in Kate's life. The Birds card appears here, so Kate will get stressed either by social media, or by the gossip she hears (or both!).

24. THE HOUSE OF HEART
the Clover card in the House of Heart predicts good fortune in Kate's romantic relationships.

26. THE HOUSE OF BOOK
the House of Book can symbolize education. The Bear card in this position may mean that Kate will educate herself so that she can make better lifestyle choices.

31. THE HOUSE OF SUN
the Home card in the House of Sun means that Kate will find happiness in her home and immediate surroundings.

34. THE HOUSE OF FISH
we can tell that money will be significant to Kate in the next three months, as the Key card has landed in this position. I would usually take this combination to mean that she should deal with pressing money matters now.

That is how you perform a general fortune reading using Lenormand cards! Next, we will look at how to perform readings on specific life areas using the Tarot.

V

—

READING
TAROT
CARDS

—

FOR LOVE,
RELATIONSHIPS
AND ROMANCE

V

Predicting your general fortune in life is always useful. However, many would-be diviners are attracted to fortune-telling because they want to know their future in specific areas of life. For example, they want to be able to answer questions about their career, spirituality and love life – and I bet you are no exception.

The most popular type of question that is asked in divination is related to love. Of the millions of people who visit my websites every year, the vast majority are looking for information about fortune-telling for relationships.

There are some methods of divination that are better suited to answering love questions than others. Lenormand cards can answer specific questions, but the system's strength lies in its ability to uncover your general fortune. At the other extreme, you can answer 'yes' or 'no' relationship questions using dowsing, but you will not get any detail from your answer.

However, Tarot cards are great for answering specific questions in detail. With one Tarot card and a good Tarot spread, you can uncover not only the past, present and future, but also other particulars, such as the strengths and weaknesses in the relationship, your true feelings about the relationship, the feelings of your lover, and so on, depending on the spread you use. A Tarot card's meaning can be interpreted in many different ways, as you can apply a card's associations in a range of spreads for a variety of types of reading. Popular questions to ask Tarot cards include:

- Will my ex-lover come back into my life?

- Will this relationship go the extra mile?

- Is that guy at work interested in me?

You can ask your Tarot cards pretty much any question that comes to mind. Once you learn how to read Tarot, the world is your oyster.

OBTAINING A TAROT DECK

The first step on your Tarot reader's journey is to purchase a deck. You do not have to buy a deck that specifically deals with love; you can get a standard Tarot deck that you can use for all your readings.

There are some very popular myths relating to Tarot reading, one of them being that you cannot buy your own Tarot deck. It is not true that your Tarot cards must be given to you for them to work. You can go into any mind, body, spirit store or hop online and purchase your first deck.

There are a range of Tarot decks on the market, and they all look very different. While it is easy to get swept away and purchase the prettiest deck, I recommend that for your first deck you get a classic Rider-Waite Tarot deck (sometimes called the Rider-Waite-Smith deck). Modern decks often rename certain elements or cards for aesthetic reasons, and this can be confusing when you are first learning Tarot, so it is best to stick to a traditional deck when you are starting out.

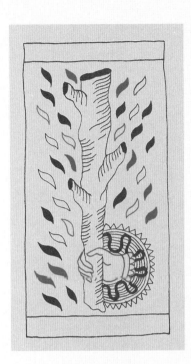

LEARNING THE
STRUCTURE OF
THE TAROT

Once you have purchased your Tarot deck, you can start familiarizing yourself with the structure of Tarot. Although some decks may rename a card or two, the basic structure of the Tarot is always the same. If your deck is not structured like the traditional Tarot, it is not a Tarot deck.

A Tarot deck is split into two main sections: the Major Arcana and the Minor Arcana. The Major Arcana contains 22 cards. Traditionally, the numbers on the Tarot cards appear in roman numerals. The Major Arcana cards are numbered from zero (0), The Fool, to twenty-one (XXI), The World. The Minor Arcana is made up of Tarot's remaining 56 cards. The structure of the Minor Arcana is very similar to the structure of playing cards, but with an extra court card. These cards are divided into four suits: Wands, Cups, Swords and Pentacles. Each suit contains ten cards numbered from ace to ten (X), and four court cards – the Page, Knight, Queen and King of the suit.

Each Tarot suit represents a different theme, but every card also has its own meaning. Each spread and combination of cards will also confer additional layers of meaning. So you can see how easy it is to gain a lot of information and detail from your love readings when using the Tarot system. From a Tarot reading, you can see if

other people are causing problems in your relationship and if a situation is going to be easy for you to change, and so on.

THE TAROT MEANINGS

Tarot meanings have evolved over time, but most interpretations are based on a book written in 1785 called *How to Entertain Yourself with the Deck of Cards Called Tarot* by an occultist named Jean-Baptiste Alliette (also known as Etteilla). Since 1911, modern Tarot meanings have been heavily influenced by *The Pictorial Key to the Tarot*, which was written by A. E. Waite – the creator of the popular Rider-Waite Tarot deck.

Most Tarot readers would agree with the basic Tarot meanings, but how diviners interpret those meanings varies from person to person. For example, some readers love the childish spirit of the Fool, while others associate this card with a refusal to grow up. So you may find yourself at odds with another Tarot reader about the implications of a card's meaning. Do not worry, as divination is a personal and intuitive process.

Here, you will find a simplified list of the Tarot card meanings for beginners. Along with learning these meanings, I also encourage you to engage with the imagery on your deck. You will notice that the depictions on Tarot cards can give you clues to the card meanings, and this will make interpreting your cards much easier.

THE MAJOR ARCANA

Many diviners interpret the Major Arcana as symbolizing major life events. The Majors also predict situations in your relationship that are very hard for you to avoid or change.

0. THE FOOL:
immaturity and playfulness.

I. THE MAGICIAN:
manifestation, skill, diplomacy.

II. THE HIGH PRIESTESS:
psychic ability, intuition, secrets.

III. THE EMPRESS:
pregnancy, feminine gender roles, mother figures.

IV. THE EMPEROR:
authority, male gender roles, father figures.

V. THE HIEROPHANT:
tradition, religion, marriage.

VI. THE LOVERS:
true love, soulmates, sexuality, choice.

VII. THE CHARIOT:
drive, willpower, fame.

VIII. STRENGTH:
power, care, tenderness.

IX. THE HERMIT:
being left on your own, loneliness, solitude.

X. THE WHEEL
OF FORTUNE:
good luck, fortune, destiny.

XI. JUSTICE:
law, morals, equity.

XII. THE HANGED MAN:
walking a tightrope, sacrifices, uncertainty.

XIII. DEATH:
endings, changes,
metamorphosis.

XIV. TEMPERANCE:
peace, contentment,
a tranquil home life.

XV. THE DEVIL:
addiction, carnal desires,
deadly sins, evil.

XVI. THE TOWER:
major breakdowns, divorce,
bankruptcy.

XVII. THE STAR:
hope, wishes, getting what
you need but not what you
expect.

XVIII. THE MOON:
the unknown, nothing as
it seems, the occult.

XIX. THE SUN:
success, happiness, holidays.

XX. JUDGEMENT:
urgency, results, verdict.

XXI. THE WORLD:
end of one cycle, start of
another, completion, travel.

THE MINOR ARCANA

Many Tarot readers interpret the Minor Arcana as representing life events that are less significant than those symbolized by the Major Arcana, but I am of the opinion that all events that pop up in your readings are important. However, Minor Arcana cards do symbolize situations that are easier to change or bend to your will. The court cards can represent you, aspects of your personality, your friends, family members, lovers or other people in your life.

WANDS

The Wands generally represent your hobbies, interests, friendships, competitions and drive. While the Wands suit is not overly dire, some of the cards do symbolize challenges.

ACE: the start of a new hobby or interest.

II: a balance of friendships and the start of partnerships.

III: the formation of groups, usually in a social or creative context.

IV: calm in your home, a good home life.

V: an exciting challenge, taking part in a competition.

VI: victory over your enemies.

VII: arguments with a group of friends, family or associates.

VIII: talking, communication and, in modern times, texting and social media.

IX: being injured emotionally or physically, feeling defensive.

X: a time of great stress and hard work.

PAGE: a person who is a strong starter but rarely finishes anything; they are excitable and easily bored.

KNIGHT: an individual who quickly enters and exits your life; they are energetic and impulsive.

QUEEN: a woman who is nature-loving, friendly and social.

KING: a man who is passionate about his hobbies, has strong leadership skills and is goal-orientated.

CUPS

The Cups suit represents your love life, romance, feelings, fertility and family. While there are one or two cards that can be considered negative, most of the Cups cards are welcome omens, especially in love readings.

ACE: the start of a new romance.

II: a well-balanced relationship, feelings of love.

III: fun with friends; attending baptisms, weddings and parties.

IV: boredom with your relationships and life in general.

V: sadness in your relationships; a traditional break-up card.

VI: remembering people from the past, the return of ex-lovers.

VII: having lots of choices, weighing up your options.

VIII: walking away from relationships that no longer serve you.

IX: the card of wish fulfilment.

X: a fairy-tale ending, relationships that get more serious.

PAGE: a loving person who often craves attention, with an idealistic view of the world and a reputation for being immature at times.

KNIGHT: a romantic individual and a knight-in-shining-armour character who sweeps their lovers off their feet.

QUEEN: a loving woman who is very empathetic and often overlooks the shortcomings of the people she cares for.

KING: a man who is very loyal to individuals in his inner circle, and who has strong psychic abilities and easily picks up on the undertones of any situation.

SWORDS

The Swords suit represents heartache, drama, conflict, misfortune and logic. Most Tarot readers view the Swords cards as unfortunate.

ACE: the start of a conflict.

II: a conflict with an equally matched opponent.

III: heartache and infidelity.

IV: a break from conflict; a period of rest.

V: playing unfair; the defeat of an enemy.

VI: movement away from drama, short-term travel.

VII: shady behaviour that you or someone else gets away with.

VIII: feeling restricted by a person or situation.

IX: anxiety, stress and sleepless nights.

X: complete ruin and drama.

PAGE: a person who loves to eavesdrop on other people's conversations; a well-known gossiper, they like to learn everything they can about their peers and associates.

KNIGHT: an individual who is quick to anger and violence; although this person has a reputation for bravery, they are extreme in everything they do and this attitude often lands them in hot water.

QUEEN: a woman who
is very hard to get along
with because she doesn't
play fair; she is a very harsh
judge of other people and is
often interpreted as an evil
stepmother or mother-in-
law character.

KING: a man who craves
power and who is very
intelligent and prefers
logic over emotions; this
individual often uses their
intellect to manipulate
people.

PENTACLES

The Pentacles suit represents your money, business, assets, education,
time and valuables. While the Pentacles is the suit of materialism,
the cards are generally quite fortunate.

ACE: the start of a new job
or business; or education.

II: a need to balance money,
time and other resources.

III: learning a new skill.

IV: hoarding money, time
and energy.

V: the poverty card –
predicts a significant
financial loss.

VI: being a giver or receiver
of charity.

VII: planning for the future.

VIII: becoming a master
of a skill.

IX: making large purchases such as a new kitchen, car or furnishings.

X: the wealth card – predicts that you will have enough money to pass to your family.

PAGE: a person who loves to learn and is the eternal student; they may not have many resources but they have big plans and aim to be successful in life.

KNIGHT: a reliable individual who likes to take their time on tasks, is consistent and dedicated, and does everything to the best of their ability.

QUEEN: a woman who loves luxury and enjoys the finer things in life, and who likes to invest her time, money, feelings and other resources wisely.

KING: a hard-working man who likes to save his money and hates time-wasters; he especially values tradition, but his views can be classed as outdated.

A NOTE ABOUT REVERSALS

The card meanings I have given are so-called upright card meanings, but you will find some readers who also read something called 'reversals'. A proportion of readers will turn half of their deck upside down and mix them with the rest of the deck, which remains upright – this results in half of the deck images appearing the wrong way around.

I do not recommend that you use reversals. There is no standard way of reading reversals, so using them can make interpreting your cards much harder and a lot more confusing. Reading all your cards upright means that you are a lot less likely to second-guess your interpretations.

TAROT SPREADS

The Tarot is like the Lenormand system in that the cards are read using spreads. While there are only several traditional Lenormand spreads, there are thousands of Tarot spreads that you can use for relationship readings.

You will discover an array of Tarot spreads in books and online. If you cannot find a spread that fulfils all your needs, you can even design your own. Here, will show you a spread that you can use to uncover all aspects of love and relationships.

THE LOVE TAROT SPREAD

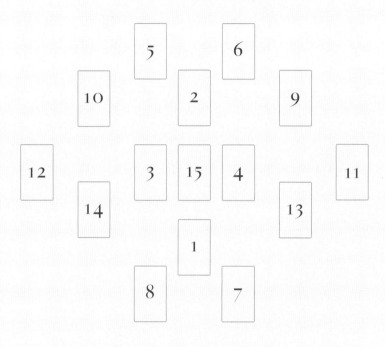

Here is a breakdown of the positions in this spread, and what they signify:

1. The Past
2. The Present
3. Your Feelings
4. Your Partner's Feelings
5. Positives
6. Negatives
7. Hopes
8. Fears
9. What to Aim For
10. What to Avoid
11. Environmental Factors
12. Other People
13. Action to Take
14. Unknown Factors
15. The Future

HOW TO PERFORM A TAROT READING

———

PREPARE FOR YOUR READING

The first steps in performing a reading are very similar for any method of divination. First, you should ask your ancestors for assistance. Next, record your questions or intentions.

PREPARE YOUR CARDS

Shuffle your cards and lay them out in the spread as shown on page 85. As you lay them out, take them from the top of the pack. The first card you put down should be in position 1, the second in position 2, and so on – until you have laid out the 15 cards required for this spread.

INTERPRET YOUR SPREAD

Interpret each card in its position in the spread. I recommend that you read the cards in order, so that you do not get overwhelmed;

this is especially important if the reading relates to a situation in which you're heavily emotionally invested.

When interpreting a love spread, especially for yourself, be mindful of your default reaction to good or bad news. Always try to go past your first reaction, tap into your intuition and ask yourself, 'What can I do now that I know this is going to happen?' Remember, your intuition will always give you options!

For the purposes of this exercise, let's pretend that we have a seeker, Maya. Maya wishes to know more about her relationship with Thomas. Here is Maya's reading and her interpretation:

THE PAST: SIX OF WANDS

The Past position reflects the past of Maya and Thomas's relationship. In the past, Maya became victorious over an enemy. Is it possible that Thomas was in a relationship with someone else when he met Maya?

THE PRESENT: SEVEN OF PENTACLES

The Present position shows where Maya and Thomas are currently in their relationship. At present, Maya and Thomas are thinking about their future and making plans.

YOUR FEELINGS: NINE OF WANDS

The third position reveals Maya's current feelings towards her partner and their relationship. Maya is afraid of getting hurt, and she is trying to avoid getting swept up in the excitement.

YOUR PARTNER'S FEELINGS: TWO OF CUPS

The fourth position reflects Thomas's current feelings towards Maya and their relationship. Thomas is happier than Maya. He loves her and feels she may be 'the one'.

V

POSITIVES: THE HIGH PRIESTESS

The Positives position shows what's helping the relationship survive. Maya is using her intuition to navigate the relationship successfully.

NEGATIVES: THE FOOL

The Negatives position shows aspects that are threatening the partnership. Maya has a playful attitude towards the relationship – she may not be able to commit properly.

HOPES: STRENGTH

The Hopes position reflects Maya's hopes for the partnership. Although Maya is apprehensive about this relationship, she does hope that she and Thomas will care for each other.

FEARS: THE EMPRESS

The Fears position reveals Maya's fears for the partnership. Maya fears pregnancy, as she is not ready for this stage.

WHAT TO AIM FOR: THE EMPEROR

The ninth position shows what Maya should be aiming for with regards to relationships. She should be aiming for someone who is able and willing to take care of her.

WHAT TO AVOID: KNIGHT OF WANDS

The tenth position shows what Maya should be avoiding with regards to relationships. Maya should avoid young men who are too focused on their friends.

ENVIRONMENTAL FACTORS: PAGE OF CUPS

Environmental factors are anything external that is affecting the relationship, such as family, work, friends or life stresses. In Maya's environment, there is a loving younger person who has influenced her relationship with Thomas. Intuitively, I feel that this may be a child of either Maya's or Thomas'.

OTHER PEOPLE: SIX OF CUPS

The twelfth position reveals what other people feel about the relationship. Maya's friends and family would rather see her back with her ex-lover.

ACTIONS TO TAKE: SEVEN OF CUPS

From this position you can see what Maya should do to make her situation better. Maya should spend some time outside her relationship until she decides what she wants from Thomas.

UNKNOWN FACTORS: SIX OF SWORDS

The fourteenth position of the Love Tarot Spread symbolizes relationship factors that are unknown to Maya. Unbeknownst to Maya, she will soon have a short break from Thomas as one of them will need to travel.

THE FUTURE: TEN OF CUPS

The final position of this spread predicts the future of Maya and Thomas's relationship. It seems as though Maya and Thomas's relationship will get more serious, despite her current anxiety. Maya and Thomas will be happy in the future.

That is how to perform a full Tarot reading for your love life and romantic relationships. As you can see, although you can learn the basic meanings, you have to interpret those meanings based on your own circumstances and intuition – so this is something we are going to look at next.

VI

CRYSTALS

FOR CONNECTING
TO YOUR
INTUITION

rystal healers work with the energetic properties of crystals to improve our physical and emotional wellbeing. However, you can also use small crystals, known as tumbled stones, for fortune-telling. In both healing and spiritual practices, crystals have well-known attributes and properties that you can adapt for divination. In everyday life, we often use the terms 'meaning' and 'interpretation' interchangeably, but they are different in divination. A 'meaning' is the symbol's pure and basic endowment. For example, rose quartz is associated with love. 'Interpretation' refers to how a symbol is understood with regards to a specific question, reading, the position in a spread, other symbols and the diviner's impressions. So rose quartz, which symbolizes love, could be interpreted as signifying a romance at work in a career reading, or self-love in a personal context, or platonic love when it comes to friendships or family. The results of divination are always subject to interpretation. Forming accurate interpretations is something you will begin to do as you become more experienced.

The use of crystals or stones for divination is known as lithomancy. There are two methods that you can use. The first involves casting crystals on to a board and reading how they fall. The second method requires you to select a crystal randomly from a bag or pouch – and this is the method that you will learn here. (We will cover casting in Chapter 13.)

If you already know a bit about crystal healing, you can adopt the holistic properties of crystals into your divination practice. Here we are going to focus on the colours of crystals and their associated meanings. You can also apply these colour meanings to other methods of divination, such as dream interpretation.

Like other methods of divination, you can use crystals for readings on a range of life concerns. You can ask your crystals questions about love, friends and family, for example; but crystals really shine when predicting matters relating to careers.

Crystals are best suited for career readings because many outside factors can impact your career, and vice versa. If you were performing a career reading today and you pulled an orange crystal, this could mean that a desire for fun will affect your work. Another crystal could mean that your work will affect your relationships, and so on.

CRYSTAL MEANINGS

Crystals of the same colour often have similar meanings, and this is true whether you are using crystals for healing or divination. Once you know the attributes of a particular colour, you can apply this to a range of crystals.

RED
Commonly used: red jasper, garnet and carnelian.

This is the colour of blood, so good for health and vitality. Pulling a red crystal can predict that you will avoid an illness that is going around your workplace. Another interpretation could be that you will find the strength to get through the day.

Red is also a colour that diviners associate with passion. While pink symbolizes softness, red is fierier and represents sexual tension. Therefore, red can predict a no-strings-attached affair in the workplace.

PINK

Commonly used: morganite, rose quartz and lepidolite.

Pink is the colour of emotional love. Pink predicts romantic feelings and pure intentions that are not always sexual in nature. For career readings, a pink crystal can predict that you will work on a project that you love.

Although pink is strongly associated with romance, it is also the colour of platonic friendships. When pulled for divination, a pink crystal can predict that you will work well with others and even make new friends.

ORANGE

Commonly used: peach aventurine, orange calcite and amber.

Orange is another friendship colour. While pink symbolizes friendships based on mutual care, orange symbolizes friendships based on a shared sense of humour, hobbies and interests. Pulling an orange crystal foretells fun and community in the workplace.

Orange is also a colour of encouragement. Orange says, 'You can do this, it'll be fun!' Orange crystals can predict motivation and being stimulated at work.

YELLOW

Commonly used: citrine, yellow jasper and golden haematoid.

Yellow is the colour of education. It is very common to pull a yellow crystal for a work-related reading, as yellow can predict that you will soon learn something new. Your crystals are telling you that today you are going to increase your knowledge.

Yellow is also a colour that humans and nature have come to

associate with danger. Yellow crystals can therefore be a warning that you should avoid rocking the boat.

GREEN
Commonly used: aventurine, malachite and chrysoprase.

Green is probably the best colour crystal you can pull for a career reading. Green crystals can predict an increase in wages. Green crystals can also mean that you will see an increase in work projects in general, especially if you're self-employed.

While green is a great colour for career readings, it is also the colour of envy and the seven deadly sins. Sometimes green can serve as a warning not to boast of your good fortune. For career readings, green is a sign that you should keep your pride to yourself.

BLUE
Commonly used: lapis lazuli, aquamarine and larimar.

In most mystical traditions, blue is the colour of truth. If you have been waiting for the truth to come out with regards to a particular situation at work, pulling a blue crystal during your divination means that all will soon be revealed.

If your work life has been stressful, receiving a blue crystal is a good sign, because blue is also associated with peace. So, while the truth is exposed with blue, it will happen in a way that will not upset the tranquillity in your office.

Finally, the colour blue can symbolize good communication; in crystal healing, blue crystals are used to strengthen the throat chakra (first described in detail by the ancient Hindus, the chakras are vortexes of energy situated at fixed points within the body). If you do not feel as though you're being heard at work, blue crystals can mean that you will soon conjure up the strength to express yourself better.

PURPLE
Commonly used: amethyst, iolite and charoite.

Purple is the colour of psychic ability. If you pull a purple crystal, it can mean that you will get the opportunity to exercise your intuition in the workplace and navigate a particular situation.

For career readings, purple is a very good colour because it is also associated with royalty and nobility. Therefore, if you pull a purple crystal this can predict a promotion or change in status at work.

BROWN
Commonly used: tiger's eye, smoky quartz and aragonite.

Brown is the colour of growth. Because this colour is found a lot in nature, brown crystals are considered by diviners to be good omens for those people who wish to develop and grow through their careers.

Both brown and black are ancestral colours. To pull a brown crystal can mean that your ancestors are around, supporting you through the good and bad times in your career. Brown is an especially positive colour for people who work with animals or nature.

BLACK
Commonly used: obsidian, onyx and black tourmaline.

If there is someone in your workplace whom you would like to see gone, you should hope that you pull a black crystal during your divination. Black is the colour of banishment. In magical traditions, black is used when the magician wishes to clear an energy, person or situation out of someone's life.

Black is also the colour of moral justice. Black can predict that you or someone in your workplace will receive their just deserts – whether this is positive or negative for you depends on your past behaviour.

WHITE

Commonly used: white howlite, quartz and moonstone.

White is similar to black in that it is used to clean and clear: first black banishes energies and then white purifies the space. Therefore, white or clear crystals can predict new beginnings.

Both black and white symbolize morals and ethics. However, while black is associated with getting even, white represents just behaviour. To pull a white crystal means that you should take the moral high ground, even in work situations where doing so is difficult.

GREY

Commonly used: grey banded agate, haematite and Preseli bluestone.

The colour grey is between black and white, and therefore most diviners interpret it as symbolizing an in-between state. Pulling a grey crystal can also mean that your workday will be uneventful. You can expect the same old, same old.

However, grey is an extremely fortunate colour to receive if your work requires creativity. Grey is the colour of innovation, predicting that you are going to come up with something cutting-edge and original.

HOW TO PERFORM A CRYSTAL READING

OBTAIN YOUR CRYSTALS

The first step in performing lithomancy is to purchase your crystals if you do not already own any. For the purposes of lithomancy, it is best if you purchase thumbled (also known as tumbled) stones. Thumbled stones are small, polished crystals. They are best because they will not get chipped or broken in the way that raw crystals might. Also, the colours of raw crystals are often not as vibrant as those of shaped and polished stones.

When crystal shopping, be mindful that some stones can appear in a range of colours; this is most common with warm-coloured crystals. Depending on composition, grade, environment, etc., one carnelian crystal may look more orange, while another carnelian could appear a very deep red.

If you think that sometimes your crystal looks brown, but sometimes it looks black, you may second-guess yourself when you're interpreting the crystal for a reading. Make sure you're clear about the colours of your crystals before you start using them for divination.

It is ideal if you can purchase crystals of roughly the same size so that you cannot tell them apart when you select them from your pouch (see below). For this form of divination, you're supposed to be blindly selecting a crystal. Over time, you can become accustomed to the size and feel of your individual crystals and this can cause you to pick out the crystals you want to receive, making your divination obsolete.

I recommend that you purchase your crystals in person from a mind, body, spirit shop if you can, instead of online. Doing so will ensure that you get the right shade/colour of crystal and that all your crystals are approximately the same size. You may want to choose a crystal you feel energetically drawn to. When you purchase from a store, you have a chance to handle all the crystals and discern which one 'speaks' to you .

Some crystals are more challenging to find than others – for example, it is easier to find jasper than it is to find larimar – and some are more costly than others. The important thing is that you find crystals in each of the colours we have covered.

SELECT YOUR POUCH

You can use any small bag or pouch for lithomancy as long as you cannot see through it. I have found that small drawstring bags are best. Once you assign a bag to be for lithomancy divination, you should keep it especially for this purpose with your lithomancy crystals stored safely in it.

SELECT YOUR
CRYSTAL

Before you start work, put all your crystals in your bag and shake them. While you are mixing up your crystals, think of your issues at work. As always, ask your ancestors to help you perform the best possible reading.

When you feel ready, without looking inside, open your pouch. Put your hand in and pull out a crystal. Interpret the message.

Let's say that our seeker, Damian, works in a coffee shop and wants to know more about what the day has in store for him. He asks, 'What is going to happen at work today?' For Damian, we pull a haematite crystal. As Damian's crystal is grey, we can say that, for today at least, nothing worth noting is going to happen at work.

Then Damian informs us that next month he is leaving his current position and is going to step into a promotion. He asks us to pull a crystal and predict what the future holds. We pull a malachite, which is a green crystal. We can tell Damian that his new position will be financially abundant. However, he should not rub his promotion in the faces of other staff members.

Through lithomancy, you can make predictions about different facets of your career or business. However, for many people, their career may be going well, but money can still be tight. What if you would like to know more about your finances in particular? We will turn to this next.

VII

NUMER-
OLOGY

FOR MONEY AND
FINANCES

Numbers are of great importance to diviners, probably even more than colour. As a diviner, it is always a good idea to pick up as much information as you can about the meanings of numbers. The system of divination that assigns special significance to numbers is called numerology. While divination is no substitute for professional or legal advice, it is a fun way to predict future events. Using numerology for financial matters is an obvious choice, as both subjects rely heavily on numbers.

There are different methods of numerology. There is 'true' numerology, which gives special meaning to numbers, and arithmancy, a system that breaks down names into numbers and percentages. The fun thing about numerology is that not only can you interpret the meaning of names and dates, but also you can use the power of numbers to make better decisions. Through numerology you can manifest the life you desire.

NUMBER MEANINGS

Regardless of which method of numerology you use, numbers always have the same meanings in divination. Technically, all numbers from zero to infinity have individual meanings, but most diviners will break a number down to a single digit and the three master numbers. This means that you only have to know the meanings of the numbers 1 to 9, and the master numbers 11, 22 and 33. Master numbers are considered the most powerful numbers in numerology. If you get a number bigger than 9 that is not a master number, such as 12, add that number's individual digits together (in this case, 1 + 2) to form a single number (1 + 2 = 3).

Here are the meanings of numbers 1 to 9 and the master numbers.

1

This is the number of leadership, rule and influence. The 1 is mainly associated with men and male energy. In a financial reading, it can predict that you will gain control of your finances. If you want to take charge of your purse strings, 1 is a good number.

2

The 2 is the number of opposites, but also equilibrium. At best, 2 symbolizes peace and at worst it predicts extremes. The number 2 is associated with women and feminine energy. This is a good number if you're trying to be more balanced with your finances.

3

The number 3 is the number of families. In divination, the number 3 often predicts childbirth and fertility. In general, it is also the number of creativity and fun, and often predicts group gatherings. If you're saving money for social reasons, or because you have a wedding, baptism or party coming up, 3 is the number you should use.

4

This is a logical number that is associated with problem-solving and reasoning. In some cases, 4 can symbolize houses and architecture. If you're struggling with a financial issue, 4 is a good number. Alternatively, if you're saving for a house or anything connected to buildings, you will also want to incorporate the number 4.

5

Because most people have 5 fingers and 5 toes on each hand or foot, 5 is the number of humanity. This number is also strongly associated with cultural pleasures and the creative arts. The number 5 predicts travel, adventure and beauty. If you're saving for a holiday or trip to a faraway place, 5 is the number you should be aiming for.

6

The number 6 is a sensual number, associated with love, compassion and sympathy. While friendships can be represented by 6, diviners usually take 6 to predict romantic partnerships. Therefore, if you're starting a joint bank account or saving as a couple, 6 is a good number for you.

7

The 7 is the most mystical number. It symbolizes psychic ability, intuition and spirituality. Religions can also be represented by number 7. If you're saving for something connected to your spiritual path (such as a special retreat), 7 is the number you should go for.

You can also use the number 7 if you wish to make better decisions about money. While 1 is a good number to adopt if your finances are out of control, 7 is ideal when you need to speculate financially. Therefore, 7 is the best number if you're purchasing stocks and shares.

8

The 8 is a pretty straightforward number, as it predicts drive, focus and ambition. Most diviners view it as the number of achievement, and it is considered lucky in Chinese culture. In India, the number 8 is associated with wealth. It is a good number if you're saving and investing. In some cases, 8 is also a wise choice for people who intend to spend money on tuition.

9

Finally, 9 is the number of charity and is associated with activism, hard work and consistency. The number 9 can predict that there will be one last push before you get to a goal. This number is best if you are using any money you have saved to help others.

11

During the study of spirituality, you'll often see the number 1 in sequence (in the form of 11, 111 and so on). Diviners believe numbers that contain only 1s symbolize angelic communication, heaven and divine guidance. Sequences of 1 are a sign that your guardian angel is nearby. With regards to finances, you should use the number 11 if you need divine protection for your savings or investment plans.

22

In sequence, 2s in numbers such as 22, 222 and so on are associated with creations that benefit humanity. The number 22 is the number of great change and inventions that affect the world. There are 22 books in the Avesta, the sacred book of the ancient Zoroastrian religion, and there are 22 Major Arcana cards in the Tarot and 22 letters in the Hebrew alphabet. You should deploy the number 22 if you want to use your money to encourage lasting change.

33

The 3 often appears in sequence as the number 33 or 333. Many Christians believe that 33 is the number of Christ. In numerology, 33 is associated with illumination, higher consciousness and responsibility. For these reasons, it is a good idea to adopt the number 33 into your finances for spiritual causes.

HOW TO CALCULATE YOUR LUCKY NUMBER

Using your date of birth, add the single digits of your birth day, month and year separately to generate three single-digit numbers, then add these three numbers until you get a single-digit number or master number. This is your principal lucky number, also known as your Life Path Number. For example:

$$13 . 04 . 1987$$

$$1 + 3 = 4$$

$$0 + 4 = 4$$

$$1 + 9 + 8 + 7 = 25 \rightarrow 2 + 5 = 7$$

$$4 + 4 + 7 = 15 \rightarrow 1 + 5 = 6$$

In this instance, your main lucky number is 6.

USING NUMEROLOGY FOR YOUR FINANCES

If you want to use traditional numerology to improve the fortune of your finances, the best way is to incorporate the right numbers into your plans. You can incorporate your lucky number or a number with a meaning that matches your goal.

One way is to start a savings or bank account on a date that provides a single numerological value that includes your lucky number or which is aligned to your goal. For example, if you're opening a bank account with a partner, try to do so on a date that has a numerological value of 6, such as 3 June 2022. Add the day (3) to the month (6) and year (2022):

$$3 + 6 + 2 + 0 + 2 + 2 = 15$$

As 15 is a two-digit number, reduce this further:

$$1 + 5 = 6$$

You might need to do some calculations to figure out the best date that isn't either too soon or too far into the future for you. For example, you may not want to wait a couple of years to open your bank account. In this case, you would use a different date that has the numerological value you're looking to capture.

Alternatively, you might want to use numerology to predict when to take a certain action. For example, you could arrange romantic dates or wedding days on those dates that have a numerological value of 6, plan a family birthday bash on a day that adds up to 3, or take a flight for a round-the-world trip at a time that adds up to 5.

HOW TO CALCULATE YOUR LUCKY NUMBERS USING ARITHMANCY

———

Not only can you use numerology to work out the divination value of different numbers, but also you can use arithmancy, an offshoot of numerology, to calculate the value of names. You can use your name to calculate your Life Destiny Number, another of the core lucky numbers that relate to your innate qualities.

If you have changed your name (either for personal reasons or through marriage), this will also change the numerical value of your name and, in turn, change your fortune. At the advice of a numerologist, supermodel Agyness Deyn (born Laura Hollins) changed her name to increase her chances of finding success as a model.

Using your full name and the aid of an arithmancy chart, add the numbers corresponding to the letters in your first name, mid-

THE MODERN ORACLE

dle name(s) if you have any, and surname separately to generate
three single-digit numbers. Then add these numbers until you get
a single-digit number, or master number. For example:

1	2	3	4	5	6	7	8	9
A	B	C	D	E	F	G	H	I
J	K	L	M	N	O	P	Q	R
S	T	U	V	W	X	Y	Z	

An arithmancy chart, showing the numerical value of letters in the alphabet.

Let's take the name John Smith as an example:

JOHN

$$1 + 6 + 8 + 5 = 20 \longrightarrow 2 + 0 = 2$$

SMITH

$$1 + 4 + 9 + 2 + 8 = 24 \longrightarrow 2 + 4 = 6$$

$$2 + 6 = 8$$

John Smith's Life Destiny Number is 8. This means that John is very driven, career-focused and goal-orientated. As certain cultures would consider 8 a lucky number, they might predict that John will live a fortunate life.

USING ARITHMANCY FOR YOUR FINANCES

There are several ways to use arithmancy to ensure good fortune in your finances. As well as incorporating your lucky numbers, you can calculate the numerology of words that match your goal, such as 'success' or 'dream house', and incorporate those into your plans – for example, as a savings target, a PIN or a date to start saving.

These are some of the ways you can perform readings using numbers and use numerology to improve your fortune. You will also be able to apply these number meanings to other methods of divination.

VIII

DREAM INTERPRE- TATION

FOR FRIENDS AND FOES

D ream interpretation is probably the oldest method of divination. Also known as oneiromancy, it features in the earliest records of written language. Prophetic dreams appear in both the Epic of Gilgamesh from ancient Mesopotamia and the Bible. We can safely assume that for as long as humans have dreamed, they have assigned meanings to their dreams.

Dream interpretation is very accessible. It doesn't require any tools, and you will not have to go far to find seekers who want you to interpret their dreams. Most diviners dip their toe enthusiastically into the world of dream interpretation. However, once they purchase their first, massive dream dictionary, they flick through a few pages and become overwhelmed. Many people are put off by the enormous number of symbols they have to learn. But, you can refer to the simple guide to the most common symbols at the back of this book (see 'List of Symbols and Meanings', pages 189–92), and you'll be surprised at how quickly you start to remember them, especially those symbols that appear most frequently to you.

SWEET DREAMS

Everybody dreams, but not everyone remembers their dreams. If you're the type of person who cannot recall much or any part of your dreams, there are a couple of things that you can do. Having a spiritual ritual before bed can encourage dreams. Just as you would when about to perform a reading, you can ask your ancestors to bless you with a meaningful dream.

Some people also find that spraying certain essential oils in the bedroom can help. Traditionally, lavender is associated with sleeping, but I also recommend myrrh and anise essential oils. You can diffuse them in a burner before bedtime (making sure to extinguish

any candle flames before you fall asleep), or dilute them in water and spray into the air with an atomizer. Do not spray essential oils directly on to your pillow as this can cause skin irritation and headaches.

RECORD YOUR DREAMS

When you wake from a good night's slumber, even if you can recall only tiny flashes from your dream, you should write down everything that you remember. Even glimpses of scenes, colours or symbols should be recorded.

Recording what you remember as soon as you wake up in a dream journal next to your bed will train your psyche to recall more and more detail from your dreams. Diviners find that they get a lot of detail from their dreams because they are actively hoping for information when they hit the hay. Dreams are fresh in a diviner's mind. By writing everything down, you're telling your intuition that you want to receive a message.

RECORD YOUR INTERPRETATIONS

When you write down your dream (or what you can recall of it), you should also record your interpretations. Taking note of them means that you can assess their accuracy. As time goes on and you look back on your previous interpretations, you can see where you have gone right or wrong, and this will strengthen your skill as a diviner.

HOW TO INTERPRET ANIMAL BEHAVIOUR IN DREAMS

———

You can interpret all sorts of symbols for different types of reading in dream interpretation, but here we focus on animal behaviour for the purposes of telling the fortune of friendships.

Animals appear frequently in dreams, and they often represent friends, acquaintances and family members. Animals symbolize people because we habitually associate animal behaviour with human traits. For example, we say that someone is as 'busy as a bee' or as 'quiet as a mouse'. (See pages 189–90 for a list of common animal symbols and their meanings.)

Although we are going to look specifically at animals here, you can also apply the symbols you have learned in the previous chapters to your dreams. The interpretations we have discovered for symbols such as scythes and mountains, are all relevant.

However, while it is important that you learn the meanings of symbols, they do not have much significance if you cannot interpret them. One half of performing dream interpretations is learning symbolic meanings, and the other half is interpreting them. For example, a zebra on its own could simply signal the presence of a cosmopolitan person in your life. However, if you dream that you have been trampled on by that zebra, your dream will take on a different interpretation.

The context in which the animal appears in your dream will tell you more about the future actions of the person they represent. Again, I recommend that you calibrate these meanings to your own experience, but here are some universal divination interpretations:

RUNNING

To run towards something predicts the pursuit of a dream. If you dream that a sheep is running, it means you have a playful friend who is reaching their goals.

TRANSPORT

If you see an animal on a plane, in a car or on a train, this predicts that the person it represents will rapidly advance towards their goals.

CHASE

To be chased by an animal in a dream relates to someone who is going to pursue you. If you outrun them, you will evade them in real life, but if you trip, they will have an effect on your reputation.

CAGED

To see a caged animal means that this person is going to be restricted in some way. A caged duck can mean that a person who is usually happy is being trapped by something or someone. As ducks are quite positive, seeing one in distress is clearly an unfortunate dream. However, to see a hyena caged would be good for the dreamer.

AFFECTION

If an animal has a friendly disposition towards you, this means that you will befriend a person with that animal's traits. For example, if you dream that a fox happily rubs itself up against you, or even sits on your knee, this predicts a friendship with a creative, entrepreneurial or cunning person.

DEATH

Dreaming that you kill or attack an animal means that you will attack a person with those characteristics in real life. To kill a sinister animal (such as a shark, jackal or rodent) predicts that you will triumph over your enemies. To kill a more neutral animal means that you will commit a betrayal against a person with that animal's characteristics.

SIZE

It is very common to dream of an animal that is bigger or smaller than it would be in real life. When an animal appears larger than normal, this means that the characteristics of that animal are exaggerated; for example, a large seal would symbolize an extremely humorous, entertaining person. Dreaming that an animal is smaller than usual means that their personality characteristics are still notable but minimized – so a small seal would represent someone who is funny but who only shows this side to certain people.

ATTACK

To be bitten or scratched by an animal predicts a betrayal. Dreaming that you are attacked by a dog, for instance, could mean that you will be betrayed by a close friend.

HIDING

Dreaming that an animal is hiding can mean that the person represented by that animal is sneaky in real life. It can also mean that you overlook the obvious when it comes to that particular individual. If an animal shrinks in order to hide, the same applies.

While interpreting your own dreams is great, as a reader, you should aim to branch out. Your goal should be to read for other people, so that you can gain more divination experience – and a good place to start is by reading for family members.

IX

—

TEA LEAF READING

—

FOR HOME AND FAMILY LIFE

I f you're new to divination, you're probably wondering, 'When can I start reading for other people?' There are no rules about how long you should practise before you read for others. I feel that you should try to read for other people as soon as possible, as this is the only way in which you can gain experience. I recommend that you start to read for your friends or family members, and then, having gained more experience, you will eventually be able to read for strangers.

Tasseomancy, the correct name for tea leaf divination, is a great way to practise reading for friends and family. Tea leaf readers use tea leaves and cups as tools for fortune-telling.

Although people who are unfamiliar with divination may find tea leaf reading strange, there are certain cultures that give special status to cups. For some, using teacups for mystical purposes comes naturally. In Romany Gypsy culture, for instance, we attach a lot of superstitions to teacups, so adopting them as spiritual objects

does not require a stretch of the imagination. Because cups directly touch the mouth, we treat them differently from plates or pots. When washing dishes, we observe the *marime* law that requires us to wash teacups before any other item. If you do not wash cups first and instead wash them after other items, this makes them physically and spiritually unclean. Throwing off the correct washing order can cause your cups to 'infect' whoever uses them, which can lead to everything from illness to bad luck.

Along with having rules about washing teacups, Romany Gypsies also give special care to their cups. We always store our cups above waist level (as anything below the waist is considered *marime*). If a person does not abide by *marime* laws, we store their cups separately from the cups of our family members. The cups that are reserved for *marime* people are kept under the sink.

Because we give spiritual significance to cups, using them for other spiritual reasons (such as for divination) is not difficult. However, Gypsies also do not like to use one object for two purposes as this can cause cross-contamination and therefore be *marime*. So, although we use teacups for divination, we would not use our fortune-telling teacups as a regular drinking cup.

I recommend that you purchase a teacup and use it only for divining. Not only does this ensure that your drinking teacups remain *wuzho* (physically and spiritually clean), but it also means that you can treat your divination teacup as special, just as you would your Tarot cards or dowsing pendulum. Treating your divination objects as sacred objects will cause you to take your divination more seriously.

HOW TO PERFORM A TEA LEAF READING

OBTAIN A TEACUP AND LOOSE-LEAF TEA

To perform a tea leaf reading, it does not really matter which type of tea leaves you use, but the cup can be important. You can purchase teacups that are created especially for divination. Different artists decorate their teacups based on their own artistic preferences. You can buy divination teacups that have astrology houses, Tarot cards, symbols and playing cards already marked on them.

For a specially created divination teacup, you would interpret a reading based on how your tea leaves land on the symbols painted inside the cup. However, you can just use a regular white teacup. Some people find that reading tea leaves is easier with a divination teacup, while some find it easier with a standard tea-cup. Remember, regardless of whether you use a fortune-telling or regular teacup, you should not use it for anything other than divination, as keeping your teacup just for readings will ensure that your readings feel special.

BREW THE TEA

Brew the loose tea leaves in the teacup using only water – do not add milk or sugar. Dispose of the excess water. Some diviners like their seekers to drink the tea. Others just ask their seekers to empty out the tea, without drinking it. There are some fortune-tellers who pour out the tea themselves, meaning that their seekers do not even touch the cup. Choose the method you prefer.

PETITION YOUR ANCESTORS AND SET YOUR INTENTIONS

Before the reading even begins, ask your ancestors to help you produce the best reading possible. You should petition your ancestors even if you're reading for another person. If you're reading for a relative and you share ancestors, even better!

Traditionally, tea leaf readings do not require a specific question; most offer general readings. Although you do not have to focus on a specific issue, think about your intention for the reading while executing the following instructions.

RECEIVE YOUR SYMBOLS

In a tea leaf reading, you will interpret the symbols formed by the shape of the tea leaves that are left in the cup. It is from these symbols that you can predict the future. Some people will see shapes in the tea leaves more easily than others do. If you often see symbols in clouds, you will find reading tea leaves a breeze! (Divining the future based on cloud shapes is known as nephomancy and is classed as a form of aeromancy, a system of divination performed by reading atmospheric conditions.)

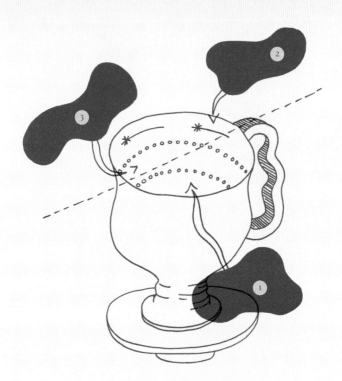

In your mind, divide the teacup into zones depicting:
1. Past 2. Present 3. Near and far events.

As with every system in this book, you can apply the symbols we have already learned to tea leaf divination. So an anchor still represents stability and a lion still symbolizes a majestic person. The 'List of Symbols and Meanings' section on pages 189–92 will provide you with further symbols and their meanings.

There are several traditions for tea leaf reading, and you will find that the instructions vary. If you find another system that you prefer, feel free to adopt it. As mentioned, divination teacups with special symbols usually have their own system of interpretation, while teacups without markings are interpreted differently.

In a plain teacup, the shapes or symbols formed by the tea leaves near the handle of the cup reveal influences that are 'close to home'. This is because your hand is closest to this part of the teacup. Anything that directly affects you, or things that you can control, will be found here.

The part of the teacup furthest from the handle, and directly opposite it, represents things that are not in your immediate environment but may still affect you. For example, a drop in the stock market is something that is happening far from your home, but it may eventually have an impact on your life.

The space between the handle and the opposite side of the teacup represents those things that are not taking place in your immediate environment but which may indirectly affect you. What this means will be different for everyone, depending on how you perceive your 'environment'. Personally, I have found the symbols that represent my friends' lives, their houses, relatives of loved ones, my workplace and places I hang out, etc., will all appear here.

The teacup is also divided vertically into present, future and distant future. The rim of the teacup symbolizes the present because it is closest to the mouth. The middle reveals the future, and the bottom of the teacup reveals the more distant future.

Finally, some diviners give special meaning to the saucer too; special divination teacups often come with saucers that also include symbols and markings. Those diviners who do use saucers typically divide the saucer into twelve 'houses', and interpret where the handle of the teacup lands when the seeker puts their teacup down on the saucer. These twelve sections hold the same meanings as the signs of the zodiac (see Chapter 11). Where the handle lands on the saucer reveals the personality of the seeker or their main concerns. For example, if the handle lands on the house of Scorpio, the seeker is concerned with sexuality, secrets and mystery. However, you do not have to use a saucer for your divination, and it is not as common to do so.

While all of this information may sound like a lot to take in, it is not that difficult once you get the hang of tea leaf reading. In fact, it is very similar to methods of card reading. Think of the symbols formed by the tea leaves as the cards and the cup as the spread. The sections of a teacup are similar to spread positions in that each reveals different aspects of the seeker's life.

INTERPRET THE READING

Once you have emptied out the water and mentally divided your teacup into zones, you must interpret your reading. Let's pretend that you have performed a reading for your sister, Lana.

If you were using a saucer, the first thing you would do is look at where the handle is in relation to the saucer. Lana has placed the teacup at a 95 degree angle on the saucer, the position of Libra. From this, we could say that, generally speaking, Lana is hoping for an easy life.

Next we would interpret the symbols in the teacup. I would interpret the top of the teacup first, as this is what is in Lana's present. On this part of the teacup, Lana has a bat symbol: this represents a person who has lived a long time, possibly a grandparent. Lana's grandparent is close to her at this time because they have landed in her 'present'. We can tell how significant this grandparent is to Lana based on the symbol's proximity to the handle.

Next, we can interpret the symbols that have landed in the mid-section of the teacup. Lana has a cross here: crosses can represent religion, but also suffering and pain. This cross is on the opposite side of the cup from the handle, so it is not in her immediate environment. Something (or someone) who is far away from Lana will soon cause her pain.

To get more detail from a symbol, we can look at the other symbols surrounding it. For example, if Lana had a heart symbol next to her cross, we could say that she will feel emotional pain because someone she loves will not be near her.

Finally, we interpret any symbols that land in the distant future position, which is the bottom third of the cup. Lana has a hand here, so we would predict that in the future, she will have to make more of an effort to achieve her goals than she is currently. A clover and a hand could mean that her efforts will result in good fortune.

It is very common to receive symbols that are obscured or damaged in some way – and this will be relevant. For example, if Lana received what looked like a hand symbol, but it was broken, we could predict that her effort will be inconsistent.

Broken or damaged body parts have the same meaning in tea leaf readings as they do in other methods of divination, such as dream interpretations. For example, several years ago I dreamed that my arm had been cut off. Not long after this, I lost my first blog (which was my livelihood) and other opportunities fell through. The broken arm predicted the loss of future opportunities.

While using tea leaves is a great way to predict events for family members, this is not to say that you can use divination only with the human members of your family. Using divination to read the minds of our furry companions is a fun exercise, and something we are going to look at next.

X

RUNES

FOR PETS AND
ANIMALS

I f you're an animal lover, you will probably feel inspired to read for your pets. Like many diviners, you may be questioning whether or not reading for your pets is possible. The answer is yes, you can indeed read for a range of animals – from dogs to crawly critters.

Animals do not have palms that we can read, and they can't tell us their dreams. However, there are other fortune-telling systems that we can adapt for animals; for example, you can read your pet's astrological birth chart or you can pull cards for them.

Even though you can use most forms of divination for animals, I believe runes are great for reading for your pets. Runes are an ancient alphabet made of symbols, and rune stones have been used in divination for centuries. Rune stones are extremely durable, so your animals cannot damage or rip them as they might Tarot or Lenormand cards. And if you lay the rune stones out on a flat surface, some pets, such as cats and parrots, can pick out their own stones – but be careful that they do not swallow them! Because your pet can choose their own runes, this system is an ideal way to read what's going on in their mind.

RUNE MEANINGS

All runes have their own keyword associations and meanings – some of which can seem somewhat contradictory. Although rune meanings will begin to make sense as you gain experience, at first it is a good idea to learn some statements that you can associate with each rune. Here are some simple rune statements that you can apply to readings for your pet:

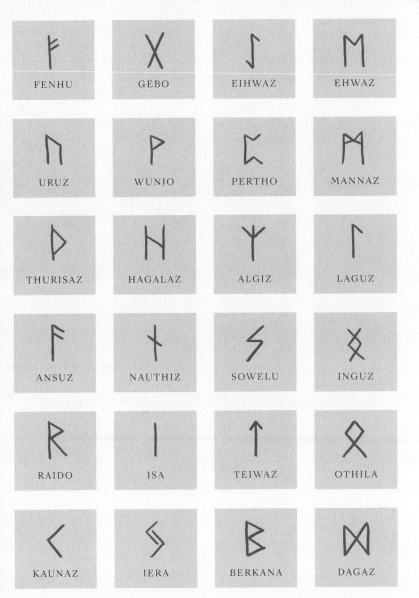

FENHU	GEBO	EIHWAZ	EHWAZ
URUZ	WUNJO	PERTHO	MANNAZ
THURISAZ	HAGALAZ	ALGIZ	LAGUZ
ANSUZ	NAUTHIZ	SOWELU	INGUZ
RAIDO	ISA	TEIWAZ	OTHILA
KAUNAZ	JERA	BERKANA	DAGAZ

FENHU
'Protect me.'

URUZ
'Don't be too aggressive
with me, but push me
to do my best.'

THURISAZ
'Today we will face
difficulties that come
out of nowhere; try to
remain vigilant.'

ANSUZ
'I am trying to communicate
with you; take notice of what
I am expressing.'

RAIDO
'I am feeling rather
adventurous today – let's
go somewhere different.'

KAUNAZ
'I don't wish to exercise
much, as I am rather
uncomfortable. However,
you could keep me
entertained in other ways.'

GEBO
'I love you and today I will
bring you something that
shows that love.'

WUNJO
'Today, I want to spend time
with you because you are my
best friend.'

HAGALAZ
'Everything currently feels
crazy. I can sense that your
happiness is out of my
hands.'

NAUTHIZ
'Give me all of your attention.'

ISA
'I am unsure of what I can
expect today. However, if it
is cold outside I am dreading
the weather so be sure to
keep me warm.'

JERA
'I am transitioning into a new
life phase; respect this.'

EIHWAZ
'Today, I wish to do activities that challenge my strength.'

PERTHO
'Be mindful of me.'

ALGIZ
'I will protect you and you should protect me.'

SOWELU
'Today is going to be a very happy day. I am feeling optimistic.'

TEIWAZ
'If I feel that another animal or person is a threat to us, I will attack them.'

BERKANA
'I am going to seek out the support and nurturing of another person or being. If I have not been spayed, and you do not want me to make babies, keep me indoors today!'

EHWAZ
'Today, all we need is each other.'

MANNAZ
'Try to remain objective today.'

LAGUZ
'Today, anything is possible.'

INGUZ
'If we try something new, it will lead to new adventures for us.'

OTHILA
'I inherited these traits from my parents, who got them from their parents. I cannot help it.'

DAGAZ
'Today, I am content with the way life is. I am looking forward to the future.'

HOW TO
READ RUNES

———

OBTAIN A SET OF RUNE STONES

Like most divination tools, runes are sold extensively online and at mind, body, spirit stores. You can buy sets made from wood or any type of stone or crystal, but the most common are made from amethyst or other stones associated with psychic development.

SELECT A RUNE FOR YOUR PET

I recommend that you choose one rune per day, per pet, as pulling too many runes can cause confusion.

There are two ways in which you can pick a rune for your pet. As mentioned, you can allow your pet to choose a rune themselves. If you decide to do this, be sure to keep a close eye on them, as some species may be tempted to pick up the runes in their mouths. Alternatively, you can select a rune on behalf of your pet.

Pick your runes as you would choose a crystal in lithomancy. Put your runes into a special pouch, shake them about and pull out the first one that comes to you: this rune will contain a message about your pet (see the Rune Meanings listed on pages 136-7).

The message you receive about your pet can be projected into
the future, or you can apply it to their present.

Most of the fortune-telling methods we have looked at so far have
concentrated on predicting the future, whether to foresee events
that lie days or months in advance. However, that is not to say you
cannot use divination to create a better life right now. Next, we look
at how to use your zodiac sign in the present to improve yourself
for tomorrow.

XI

ASTROLOGY

FOR ACHIEVING YOUR LIFESTYLE GOALS

While many diviners are attracted to divination because it helps them to predict the future, that does not mean you cannot use fortune-telling for goal-orientated readings. Every method of divination we have covered so far can predict the future and assist you with your goals and dreams. However, one of the best methods of divination for personal development is astrology.

Whether you need help with your health and fitness goals, working on your self-esteem, developing your creativity, discovering your true calling – whatever it may be – astrology can reveal a lot about your personality through your sun sign (more commonly known as your star sign or zodiac sign). If you know about your strengths and weaknesses, you can use this information to achieve your dreams and change your fortune.

The location of the sun, moon and planets in relation to the 'houses' of the zodiac at the moment of your birth forms your birth chart. Every birth chart is divided into twelve houses of the zodiac. Each house denotes a particular life area. For example, the first house represents the body and reveals your temperament. Where the planets fall in the birth chart can have an effect on this aspect of the chart.

Many factors affect your birth chart and houses, including the time you were born, the date you were born and the location of your birth. There are many free websites that will calculate your birth chart for you.

As well as your sun sign, your birth chart will reveal your moon sign, which relates to your inner emotions, and your ascendant or rising sign, which indicates how you interact with others and the outside world. It also offers a lot of other information about your personality based on the position of the planets at the exact time and place of your birth.

However, you do not have to know everything about your birth chart to be able to use it for your personal development goals. Your sun sign is enough to reveal your overall personality. The majority of your likes and dislikes, strengths and weaknesses can be uncovered by looking at where the sun is in your chart. You can then use this information to make better choices and change your future. If you work with your personality, and not against it, you will be more likely to stick to your plans.

WHAT IS YOUR SUN SIGN?

Sun signs are based on the date you were born. To work out your sun sign, simply look through the following chart and find the date you were born:

ARIES:	21 MARCH–19 APRIL
TAURUS:	20 APRIL–20 MAY
GEMINI:	21 MAY–20 JUNE
CANCER:	21 JUNE–22 JULY
LEO:	23 JULY–22 AUGUST
VIRGO:	23 AUGUST–22 SEPTEMBER
LIBRA:	23 SEPTEMBER–22 OCTOBER
SCORPIO:	23 OCTOBER–21 NOVEMBER
SAGITTARIUS:	22 NOVEMBER–21 DECEMBER
CAPRICORN:	22 DECEMBER–19 JANUARY
AQUARIUS:	20 JANUARY–18 FEBRUARY
PISCES:	19 FEBRUARY–20 MARCH

ASTROLOGY

However, please note that the dates given are approximate, as the sun does not move into each sign on the same day every year. So if you are born towards the end or beginning of a sign, close to what is known as 'the cusp', do look up your birth chart online or get a professional astrologer to draw your birth chart up for you, for an accurate reading.

HOW TO WORK
WITH YOUR
SUN SIGN

———

Based on your sun sign, you can now find out your strengths and weaknesses, and discover more about your personality. An understanding of these personality traits can help you improve your fortunes in all your life goals, but here we're going to focus on health and fitness. Astrology is a great way to increase your self-knowledge and help you to understand where in life you might be slack, what your natural talents are, and how to make sure you stick to new habits and break bad ones – perfect for helping you maintain a fit and healthy lifestyle.

ARIES

Passionate, creative, impulsive, independent, driven.

You have massive amounts of energy and a short attention span – you would rather die than feel boredom. You need high-intensity workouts to hold your interest. You would be best suited to keeping fit through an activity such as cycling or running.

When your schedule becomes too predictable, it feels burdensome and you quickly lose interest. Jogging in unknown places without a set route is your idea of a good time. While you should not risk your personal safety, be sure to push yourself further than your comfort zone.

Your competitiveness means you do not naturally work well in a team (although you will if you have to). Your desire to win and love of the extreme mean that you would do well in solo events such as running marathons or competing in triathlons.

TAURUS

Opulent, grounded, steady, practical, realistic.

You are the most decadent of the zodiac signs. Because you enjoy the finer things in life, you tend to overindulge. When Taureans want to lose weight or get healthier, most find that learning more about nutrition is the way to go.

Taureans need a meal and exercise plan that they can fit into their lifestyle. You're not the type of person who wants to devote your life to a boring jog. Instead, try going for a stroll around the shops – walking counts as exercise and an interesting environment will help to keep your interest piqued.

Like Cancerians, Taureans are natural homebodies. Taureans take pride in a well-designed environment. Gardening is a great way for you to stay fit and burn lots of calories while feeding your desire to make everything beautiful.

GEMINI

Sharing, reliable, communicative, friendly, interdependent.

As a Gemini, you do not like to be by yourself. You shine when you're part of a team. Not only do you enjoy the company of other people, but also you hate to disappoint them. You should plan exercise trips with friends or play team sports, as you're a lot more likely to succeed if your success is not just your own. Arrange gym visits, long walks or adventures with others.

It is also a good idea to sign up for gym classes such as aerobics, spinning, yoga and high-intensity workouts. If you make friends, you'll want to go to every class.

Although not particularly drawn to technology, Geminis have fun online – you use social media as a way to keep in touch with friends. If you want to live a healthier lifestyle, look for support in the form of Facebook groups or apps with a forum for members to share their workouts.

CANCER

Loyal, sentimental, emotional, protective.

Like Geminis, you enjoy intimate relationships, but you are not everybody's best friend. You despise letting loved ones down, but gaining your trust is no easy feat – those you feel obliged to help are special to you. You prefer one-on-one interaction, not group activities. You would rather attend the gym or a fitness event with a best friend, family member or lover.

As a Cancerian, you would be well-suited to swimming, especially if your local pool is not too far from your home. Again, commit to attending the pool with a partner and the time will pass much more easily for you. Cancerians are fiercely committed, so sticking to a routine is not difficult.

Crabs (the symbol of Cancer) enjoy their own shell and natural surroundings. Your home is your habitat. Home workouts and exercise DVDs would suit you fine.

LEO

Extravagant, confident, proud, generous, overbearing.

You take pride in your appearance. You'll go to the gym and eat healthily as long as you know you'll look amazing in the future. One way you can stick to a healthy lifestyle is by creating a vision board covered with pictures of your 'fitspiration'. Seeing what you can potentially look like every day will inspire you to work harder.

While you want to work out for aesthetic reasons, you do not want to look terrible while you do so. Anything that makes you sweat too much, for too long and in front of too many people will make you feel self-conscious. However, if you reward yourself with new gym gear every time you hit a goal, you can bypass any reluctance towards publicly breaking a sweat.

VIRGO

Giving, utilitarian, trustworthy, idealist, conservative.

Of all zodiac signs, you're the most likely to work in the public service or care industries. You like to give selflessly to others. Your desire to be of service to people means that you often neglect to take care of yourself. Your career can also mean that your lifestyle becomes a low priority for you. If you want to be healthier, plan your meals and pack a lunchbox to avoid eating out every lunchtime.

You spend a lot of time worrying about other people. While caring is natural for Virgos, you probably do not even realize that you do so to the detriment of your wellbeing. Practices such as meditation and mindfulness will help you control your stress.

Virgos are perfectionists. You can also be hard on yourself and often underestimate the amount of work that goes into losing weight or toning up. But, if you have a goal, you will try to achieve it at all costs – just be careful not to set yourself unrealistic targets.

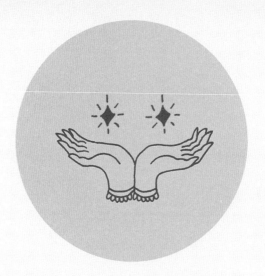

LIBRA

Fair, well-balanced, peaceful, truthful, adaptive.

You need a quiet atmosphere in your workplace, home and even gym. If you want to stick to a fitness plan, it will be best for you if you attend the gym or pool when it is not too busy.

As a Libra, you prefer to work one-on-one, not in large groups. When you're trying to change your lifestyle, you are more likely to be successful if you work with one person who is as dedicated to your success as you are. You should hire a personal trainer – they will help you to get the best results possible. Because Libras do not want any drama in their life, they have a tendency to avoid things. Having someone to help you will make you more committed to working out.

If you choose to hire a trainer, commit to block sessions of 6 or 12 weeks at a time. You want to make sure that you will stick to a new schedule, so paying in advance is a smart move.

SCORPIO

Erotic, private, ever-evolving, powerful, intense.

Scorpios have a reputation as the sexiest sign of the zodiac. As a Scorpio, you will be strongly attracted to anything that makes you feel sexy, desired and wanted. To keep fit, you should try pole dancing or burlesque.

For the Scorpio, hitting the swimming pool is an excellent choice. However, you like adventure and want to shake things up. Water sports (such as diving or snorkelling) are something you would stick to religiously.

Scorpios love mystery, secrets and solving puzzles. Get together with your friends and organize a treasure hunt or escape room – this way, you can spend the day being active without getting bored.

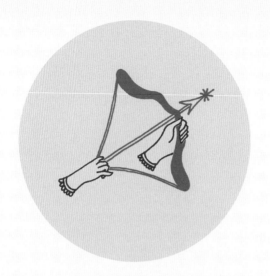

SAGITTARIUS

Ecological, spontaneous, adventurist, freedom-loving.

Sagittarians are obsessed with everything to do with nature. It would be easy for you to make your fitness goals part of your lifestyle if it means that you can be outside. You enjoy going on long walks, especially if you live near beaches or woodlands.

You would love the opportunity to be closer to animals. Dog walking, bird watching and horse riding are hobbies that you are likely to stick to. The fact that they burn extra calories is a bonus.

As a Sagittarius, you love to travel. Experiencing new foods or new sports and activities should be natural for you. Try adventure holidays, anything from snow- to sand-boarding, and you will get fit in no time.

CAPRICORN

Determined, disciplined, prudent, consistent, conventional.

Goats are the animal of the Capricorn for good reason – climbing is your thing. You have fantasies of tackling Mount Everest and have dipped your toe into hill walking in the past. You should take up mountain climbing as a way to burn your excess energy. Take the stairs instead of the elevator.

Capricorns are naturally attracted to anything that will increase their endurance. Weight lifting will ensure that you do not get bored. You need the intensity that dumbbells provide!

As a Capricorn, you take pride in pushing yourself to the point of danger. In your mind, there are no sports other than extreme sports. Try something like parkour or BMXing as a way to stay in shape and have fun doing so.

AQUARIUS

Non-conforming, analytical, unique, curious, obstructive.

As an Aquarian, you are naturally obsessed with science, astronomy, UFOs and the universe. A star-gazing camping trip is your idea of a fantasy come true. Although you might have to walk miles carrying a telescope, it would not even feel like exercise to you.

You also love to bring about change, and have a passion for social justice. Aquarians have a tendency to spend too long sitting at the computer, so organizing a political protest is a great way to stretch your legs. You would happily roam the streets all day if you were doing so in the name of liberation.

Aquarians live for conspiracy theories. You have to challenge the status quo. While this is great, you can end up adopting fad diets that are near-impossible to stick to in the long term. Try to avoid making lifestyle changes just because they are trendy.

PISCES

Receptive, poetic, talented, fluid, dreamer.

You are the most emotionally sensitive and empathetic sign of the zodiac. Because of this, you are drawn to anything mystical. You are more likely to stick to a regime if it serves your mind, body and spirit. Spiritual practices such as yoga, Pilates and tai chi are best for your sign.

Pisces are very artistic. You have to feel as though your creative juices are flowing or you will grow bored. Walks around art exhibitions or museums are great ways for you to stay fit and feed your desire for culture.

Pounding it out in the gym is not your idea of a good time. However, you are not averse to swimming, and you enjoy it more than most other signs do. Wild swimming in lakes or the ocean would suit you best. Flow freely outside in the summer and take to indoor swimming pools during the cooler months.

CREATE YOUR FITNESS PLAN

Now that you know your natural likes, dislikes, strengths and weaknesses, you can create a health and fitness plan that will work for you. Because this plan is based on your sun sign, it will be easier for you to stick to than a generic regime. You can also apply this learning about your personality to your other personal development goals. According to your sign, what's the best way for you to learn a new language, break a bad habit or save money?

While divination is great when you use it to improve your own life, you can also use it if you work in groups. If you are part of a team, divination can guide you all towards success – and this is what we are going to look at next.

XII

PALMISTRY

FOR WORKING
WITH OTHERS AND
TOGETHERNESS

A strology is not the only divination method to reveal our strengths and weaknesses. We can learn a lot about our personality by reading our palms. In this chapter, I teach you how to use palmistry to uncover how you fit into a group dynamic, the roles you take on and how you relate to others. This chapter could prove particularly useful in relation to your work life or your hobbies and interests, especially if you take part in competitive team activities such as dancing or football.

Palmistry is the art of reading the palms. There are two main branches of palmistry. The first is called chiromancy, or divination through reading the lines on the hand. This is perhaps the most famous system. By reading the lines on your hands, you can predict your future in various areas in life, such as your health, wealth and romance. To interpret the lines on the palm, you must take into account where the lines start and end, their prominence and any special marks (such as stars, spots and crosses) that appear on them.

The second form of palm reading is called chirognomy, which involves reading the personality based on the shapes of the fingers and palm, and any patterns on the mounts – those small fleshy bumps on the palm. In this chapter we will focus on chirognomy, which will reveal your natural role in a group situation and your innate abilities and talents.

Looking at the mounts on your palm will reveal key details about your personality. Traditionally, the

palms are divided into ten mounts or sections, although some diviners recognize more, some fewer. A particular trait will be more or less prevalent in you depending on whether the mount is well-defined, average or flat.

As mentioned in previous chapters, in divination, we often view signs, symbols or features as being exaggeratedly large or small. An animal can appear larger than normal in a dream, a star can appear very small in a teacup, and so on. In palmistry, the rules of size and exaggeration apply in the form of mount size. If a mount is well-defined (sometimes called overdeveloped), your personality traits represented by that mount will be extreme. If the mount is flat (sometimes called underdeveloped), these traits will be absent or lacking. Finally, mounts can also be neither well-defined nor flat but simply average or within normal range, which means that those traits are well-balanced.

You can use this information to help you find your niche and assist your team. For example, a well-defined Mount of Venus can mean that your romances affect your ability to concentrate in other areas of your life. So, if you have an overdeveloped Mount of Venus and you play for your local football team, you should curb your love dramas until the football season is over!

HOW TO PERFORM A PALMISTRY READING

WHICH PALM SHOULD I READ?

Do you read the left hand or the right hand? Many palmists prefer to read the right palm, being the hand that reflects the life you are currently living. By contrast, the left hand shows what could be and reveals any untapped potential.

In mystical traditions, the left is often associated with evil and the right with righteousness. Curses are referred to as 'left-hand work' and healing spells come under 'right-hand work'. The word 'sinister' comes from the Latin word for the left-hand side. Even in my own language, Romani, the word for left, *bango*, is the same as the word for evil; the word *bangalo* means 'devil' or 'devilish'.

There are some diviners who prefer to use the left hand for anything connected to fortune-telling. They view the left as special, unusual and therefore magical. It is not unheard of for cartomancers

The mounts of the palm.

to shuffle and cut their cards using their left hand. Personally, I do not advocate for the left or right palm. Nor do I feel that you should read only one palm during divination. I believe that the seeker will instinctively give you the correct palm during the reading. If you are your own seeker, you will check the palm that 'should' be read without even thinking twice.

You can make up your own mind about which palm you feel is the right one to use for divination. Not only will you use this hand for palmistry, but also you will need it for other fortune-telling systems.

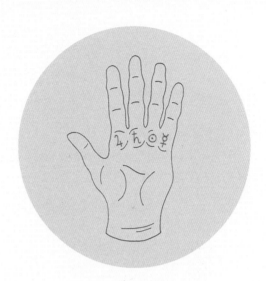

READ THE UPPER PALM

The upper part of the palm holds the first set of mounts. These are the mounts that you can find directly below the fingers. The upper palm mounts are the most important mounts for reflecting your ability to work with others.

MOUNT OF JUPITER

LOCATION: directly below the index finger.

MEANING: priorities, drive, ambition and ability to lead others.

WELL DEFINED: a well-defined Mount of Jupiter indicates very strong ambition. You prioritize your goals over everything. You must be number one and you have to lead the team. You're so driven that you tend to step over people to get what you want. You have a tendency to boss others around.

AVERAGE: if you have a normally defined Mount of Jupiter, you can take charge without being domineering. You do not have fantasies of power, but you are comfortable stepping in and leading others. You work well in a team. While you may not always have known what you want to make of your life, over time you will decide what you want to do.

FLAT: if your Mount of Jupiter area is flat, you aren't particularly ambitious. Throughout your life, you have often lacked direction. You have floated from one interest to another, unable to settle on any one subject. You've dipped your toe into many different things. You do not like to tell others what to do, and you are uncomfortable when you're put in charge of other people.

MOUNT OF SATURN

LOCATION: directly below the middle finger.

MEANING: passion, analytical skills and sense of responsibility.

WELL DEFINED: a well-defined Mount of Saturn means that you are hyper-passionate. You often get so emotionally involved that you cannot stop yourself from investing your all. You feel responsible for other people's happiness. You do 'damage control' in the lives of friends and family. Many nights you have spent lying awake, over-analysing what you could have done better.

AVERAGE: a Mount of Saturn that is not too large, but not completely flat, signifies that you have a healthy sense of responsibility. While you do recognize that your actions can affect those around you, you know that you cannot control others. You don't dwell on negatives, but you try to use them to work out how to do better next time.

FLAT: if your Mount of Saturn is flat, you are easy-going. Some people would consider you a selfish person. You avoid everything that might upset the balance of your life. Not only are you unreliable, but you also find it hard to prioritize. You do not stress over those things that you really should, and your tendency to procrastinate has affected your ability to succeed.

MOUNT OF SUN

LOCATION: directly below the ring finger.

MEANING: fame, social skills, creativity and ability to influence.

WELL DEFINED: a well-defined Mount of Sun will be found on your hand if you are a born winner. You naturally draw attention to yourself – even if you do not like to be in the spotlight. You often feel as though too much pressure is put on you by other people. You feel judged by both your wins and your failures. You have the sense that you're always expected to have new ideas.

AVERAGE: if you have a typical Mount of Sun, you are not always the centre of attention, but you do receive recognition when you deserve it. Your teammates do not expect too much of you, but they assume that you will pull your weight with regards to pitching ideas and achieving goals.

FLAT: if your Mount of Sun appears flat, you have never really felt as though you have reached your full potential. You are not particularly well known for anything, and you may even feel your life is unremarkable. You're not a winner, and you lack the ability to influence other people. You find it hard to think outside the box.

MOUNT OF MERCURY

LOCATION: directly below the little finger.

MEANING: communication, social media and tech savviness.

WELL DEFINED: a well-defined Mount of Mercury will appear on your palm if you are extremely quick-thinking. You are fast on your feet and mentally sharp. However, sometimes you rush to a decision without knowing all the facts, and your impulsive behaviour affects others and your ability to succeed. An addiction to social media may also affect your performance.

AVERAGE: do you have an average Mount of Mercury? This means that you are not too rash or too hesitant. Also, you know when to put down your phone, but you're connected to your network.

FLAT: if your Mount of Mercury is flat or non-existent, speed is not your strong point – and this is something you should work on. You often take too long to make your move. Also, you may have an aversion to social media and do not get involved.

READ THE MID-PALM

The middle parts of the palm contain your mid-palm mounts. These mounts are useful for assessing your ability to deal with confrontation and your status and role in a group dynamic.

INNER MOUNT OF MARS

LOCATION: in the area between your thumb and index finger.

MEANING: physical aggression, physical ability and rage.

WELL DEFINED: if you have a lot of loose skin around the inner thumb area, you have a well-defined Inner Mount of Mars. People with this feature may have problems with anger. You often blow up over things that your teammates would view as minor.

AVERAGE: you are level-headed. While you know that not everything can be solved with words, you would be willing to defend yourself. You do not frequently have run-ins with your teammates, and you would never threaten them.

FLAT: if you do not have much skin around your inner thumb, your Inner Mount of Mars is considered to be flat. A flat Inner Mount of Mars will typically be found on your palm if you are not a combative person. More aggressive teammates may view you as weak, and try to walk all over you. Throughout your life, people have overstepped your boundaries.

OUTER MOUNT OF MARS

LOCATION: the far middle section of the hand.

MEANING: moral aggression, bravery and willingness to do the right thing.

WELL DEFINED: if you have an overdeveloped Outer Mount of Mars, you have a tendency to sacrifice yourself for others. You often play the martyr. When things go wrong in your team, you take the blame even if you do not deserve it. Sometimes you can be judgemental of your teammates' lifestyle choices.

AVERAGE: when your Outer Mount of Mars is average, you have a strong code of ethics. You're a team player but you are not going to be the sacrificial lamb if you have done nothing wrong.

FLAT: if your Outer Mount of Mars is flat, you struggle to do the right thing. You often want to win so badly that you're willing to bend the rules. You will happily throw others under the bus if it puts you at an advantage.

PLAIN OF MARS

LOCATION: the middle section of the palm.

MEANING: commitment, self-confidence and work–life balance.

WELL DEFINED: if your Plain of Mars is fleshy, you have a tendency to be overconfident. In many areas of your life you never know when to stop. When you're working with others, you come across as being pushy and full of yourself.

AVERAGE: your Plain of Mars will be considered average if the palm of your hand is not too bony, but not too fleshy. You have a healthy level of confidence and manage to balance your hobbies with other areas of your life. You are dedicated to the things you love, but you won't force that dedication on others.

FLAT: if the middle of your palm is very bony, this means that you have a flat Plain of Mars. You lack confidence and often second-guess your ability to reach your goals. Other people feel as though they often have to pick up the slack for you. Your teammates have to voice concerns on your behalf.

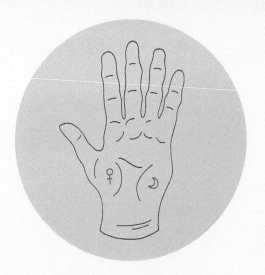

READ THE LOWER PALM

The lower part of the palm contains your lower mounts. These mounts reveal how you relate to others.

MOUNT OF VENUS

LOCATION: the thumb area on the lower part of the palm.

MEANING: reflects your affection levels, family ties and commitment to tradition.

WELL DEFINED: a well-defined Mount of Venus will be found on your hand if you are an extremely affectionate person. The health of your love life will have a massive impact on other areas of your life. If your relationships are going badly, everything else will suffer. A well-defined Mount of Venus can also mean that you can be led by a sense of family tradition or duty.

AVERAGE: if you have a typical Mount of Venus, you don't tend to allow your relationships to unsettle the rest of your life (unless you are going through something serious). You are respectful towards those who have come before you, whether these are your predecessors at work or your elders.

FLAT: a flat Mount of Venus will appear on your palm if you cannot express your feelings towards friends and colleagues. You do not show them the appreciation they deserve. You also do not respect those who have come before you – you view them as 'has-beens' who cannot teach you anything.

MOUNT OF MOON

LOCATION: directly opposite the thumb area, on the lower part of the palm.

MEANING: reflects your sense of individuality, independence, sensitivity, intuition and imagination.

WELL DEFINED: if you have a very well-defined Mount of Moon, you struggle to work in a team. You would rather work on your own. In fact, you're often attracted to activities that do not require teammates. You're also oversensitive and cannot take criticism.

AVERAGE: if you have an average Mount of Moon, you have good intuition about others but do not normally allow your psychic sense to cloud your judgement. You can work on your own or in a team.

FLAT: a flat Mount of Moon will appear on your hand if you cannot work on your own. You have to be part of something bigger than yourself. However, you must work on your intuition and empathy – you have a tendency to be self-centred.

In this chapter, we have looked at how an area of our own bodies can reveal information about us. It's time, now, to look at how to use other surfaces to bring together all that we have learned so far. Next, we will look at casting.

XIII

CASTING

FOR YOUR
ONWARD
DIVINATION
JOURNEY

Throughout this book, I have stressed that while all divination systems excel in particular life areas, there is crossover between methods. You can take what you have learned with one form of fortune-telling and apply it to another. Casting is a method of divination that involves throwing objects on to a surface and interpreting how they fall. From what you have learned so far, you will be able to build your own casting kit and perform a cast.

CASTING SYSTEMS

Casting has many sub-practices, including runes, lithomancy, charm casting and bone casting, which is known as osteomancy. While a bone diviner's kit will include bones, it may also contain sticks, shells, fossils, seeds, dice, buttons or anything small that the reader has found during their travels. Osteomancy is common among diviners who practise African Traditional Religions. Although charm casting is similar to osteomancy, charm casters use little charms for their divinations. Usually, these charms will be made for jewellery, but diviners use them for divination. Charm casting is popular in Europe.

Osteomancy and charm casting follow very different traditions; however, there are diviners who use the systems interchangeably. Some diviners will include charms, bones, dice, runes, crystals and pretty much any other small object in their casting kit.

HOW TO CREATE
A CASTING KIT

Ready-made casting kits are rare, as most diviners make their own. In modern times, many diviners source items for their kits online, or in craft shops. Even bones can be ethically sourced from the internet. However, if you're a traditionalist, your kit should consist of things you came across by chance. You may, for instance, find a fox tooth during a walk, or a nice shell on the beach. Your grandmother might give you a thimble, which you can add to your casting bag.

While items that you have found yourself will be more meaningful, I feel that your initial kit should consist of new charms you have purchased so that you can get started. As time goes on, new items will present themselves to you. If you keep objects that you have randomly come across during your day-to-day life in your casting kit, it will feel more spiritually charged. Building your kit can take years, but it will be worth it.

You can choose to use bones of animals or charms depicting animals. Your kit can also contain charms shaped like body parts, charms with numbers, or charms that include the Lenormand symbols. You can even use charms that you associate with Tarot images: cups, wands, swords and pentacles. Use your growing knowledge of symbols to select your charms.

If you wish, you can add crystals or runes to your kit. In fact, your kit may be made up entirely of runes or crystals. Your casting kit is personal to you, so build one as you see fit.

As with all your divination objects, you must treat your kit as special. You should keep it in a drawstring bag, and do not allow other people to play with your charms.

CREATE A CASTING BOARD

As with most divination practices, there are differing traditions. Some diviners will simply interpret their readings based on how the items fall, while others will use a casting board or cloth with markings and interpret the charms in relation to the symbols on which they fall.

If you're just starting out, a casting board is ideal, because it can give you more context as to how to interpret the way your charms have landed. You can buy a board online, or you can make your own.

Casting boards can be made from card, wood or cloth. In fact, your board does not even have to be a real board; just as with tea leaf reading, you can mentally divide a surface to create an imaginary board. You can even mark a surface in chalk; in fact, this practice is relatively common.

While you can assign any meanings you want to your board sections, to get the most from your divination journey I recommend that you divide your area into twelve sections (like a pie) and assign a sun sign to each area. Your interpretations for each section will vary depending on what your goal is for your reading. While you should use a large board for casting, you can create a smaller board with the same attributes for a system such as dowsing.

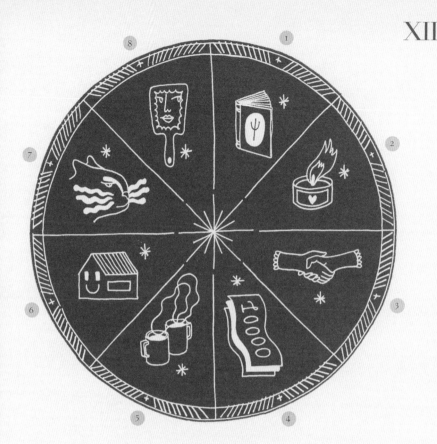

The sections on a casting board and what they signify.

1. Psychic and spiritual development.
2. Love and relationships.
3. Career or business.
4. Money, finances and resources.
5. Friendships.
6. Family and home.
7. Pets and animals.
8. Health, wellness and personal goals.

CASTING

PETITION YOUR ANCESTORS

As you should with all readings, remember to petition your ancestors and ask them to assist you with your reading.

CAST YOUR ITEMS

To cast, take your charms, bones, crystals and other objects in your preferred hand. If you do not have a preference, just pick up your items with either hand (or both hands if your kit contains a lot of items).

While holding your items, try to think only of your intention. For this first cast, your intention is to reveal how you can make the most from your divination journey.

If you're having trouble clearing your mind, you can place a crystal ball in close proximity, which you can look into. Staring into a crystal ball can help you to get into a meditative state (see Chapter 2). You can do this for any type of reading.

When you are ready, throw your items on to your casting area.

INTERPRET THE READING

Let's say that I have a kit made up of the following items:

SHARK'S TOOTH: sharks symbolize hurtful people. Because the shark's tooth has landed in the friendship part of the board, I can say this predicts that I will soon be emotionally harmed by a close friend.

CHARM WITH THE NUMBER 3: this has also landed on the friendship part of the board. Because 3 is the number of family and pregnancy, I believe this predicts that one of my friends is soon going to have a baby.

ANCHOR CHARM: this has landed on the section of the board that represents money and finances. Because the anchor is associated with consistency, this means that my finances will be secure in the future.

LARIMAR CRYSTAL: larimar is a blue crystal that is associated with self-expression. This has landed in the animal part of the board, which signifies that I often voice my opinions to my pets.

FINGER CHARM: fingers are associated with ideas. As the finger charm has landed on the business and career part of the board, this means that I receive lots of good ideas for my business.

OTHILA RUNE: this has landed in the family and home part of the board. I have inherited many of my skills from my family. The next generation will inherit them from me.

BEAR CLAW: bears can symbolize authority figures (especially mothers), weight and lifestyle. However, this has landed outside the board.

There will be times when your casting items fall outside the board. There are different interpretations as to what this means, but sometimes it can predict that the issues represented by that item cannot be revealed to you. For example, in my reading, part of a bear claw did not land on the board. We could say that it fell outside the board because I am not meant to know the impact my lifestyle has on me at the moment. Alternatively, we could say that it means that the subjects it represents have no impact on my life in the near future.

Finally, there will be times when nothing lands in certain parts of the board – this phenomenon can also happen in astrological birth charts when the houses are 'empty'. In divination, this means that those areas of your life are not your main concern. In the reading of mine that I have been describing, nothing lands in the health and wellness part of the board. I can say that I am not overly focused on my health. Having empty houses can either be viewed as areas of advantage or places where you can improve, depending on how you interpret them.

Creating your own casting kit is an important milestone in your divination journey. Over the years, you may add pieces, remove features and even change everything. However, one thing is for sure: this is a journey that will hold many more surprises and discoveries for you on your way to becoming a diviner.

CONCLUSION: BECOMING A DIVINER

I sincerely hope this book has opened the door for you to many new and wonderful methods of divination. You are no longer a newbie, but well on your way to becoming a confident diviner who is well-versed in many different methods of divination.

You can take what you have learned in this book and build upon your newfound knowledge. Hopefully, you have discovered a fortune-telling system (or two) that speaks to you. You can now move on to learn more meanings and apply the divination methods in this book to many different areas of life.

Remember, being a diviner is a path for life. As diviners, we never stop learning – we only build on and refine our skills. With time and practice, you too will soon become the oracle you have dreamed you can become. Good luck on your divination journey!

THE A–Z OF DIVINATION

If you have mastered the methods of divination in this book, you might want to explore other techniques of fortune-telling and predicting the future. In this brief guide, you will find alternative forms of divination as well as some now familiar systems.

AEROMANCY: a method of divination that involves interpreting changes in the weather as a precursor to events.

APANTOMANCY: a form of divination that gives special meaning to signs and symbols that the diviner comes across in their day-to-day life. (See Chapter 1.)

ASTROLOGY: a method of divination that gives special significance to the position of stars, planets and other heavenly bodies. (See Chapter 11.)

AUGURY: a type of divination that involves interpreting the movement of birds as they fly or pick at corn.

AUTOMATIC WRITING: a method of divination that requires the diviner to clear their mind and write down the messages they receive intuitively, without thinking about the process.

BIBLIOMANCY: a system of divination that involves interpreting the meaning of passages or pages opened at random in a book. To practise bibliomancy, simply take a book, ask for guidance, open at a random page and begin reading. Many people who practise bibliomancy use the Bible or other religious texts.

CARTOMANCY: methods of divination that use cards (including Tarot and Lenormand; see Chapters 4 and 5). However, the term often refers to divination using regular playing cards.

CASTING: forms of divination that involve throwing down items and interpreting how they fall. (See Chapter 13.)

CHIROGNOMY: a type of palmistry that focuses on interpreting the mounts, fingers and shape of the hand. (See Chapter 12.)

CHIROMANCY: a form of palmistry that focuses on interpreting the lines and marks on the hand. (See Chapter 12 for a brief description.)

CLEDONISM: a method of divination that gives special meaning to those words and phrases that the diviner comes across in their day-to-day life.

DOWSING: a kind of divination that uses crystals or wood suspended from a string. The direction in which this string sways will reveal the future. (See Chapter 3.)

LENORMAND: a method of divination that uses 36 cards based on symbols taken from everyday life. (See Chapter 4.)

LITHOMANCY: a type of divination that involves assigning meaning to crystals and then randomly selecting those crystals as a means of predicting the future. (See Chapter 6.)

NEPHOMANCY: a form of aeromancy that involves interpreting the shapes in clouds.

NUMEROLOGY: a method of divination that gives

special meaning to numbers. (See Chapter 7.)

ONEIROMANCY: the correct name for dream interpretation or divination through interpreting dreams. (See Chapter 8.)

ORACLE CARDS: cards that are used for divination, but which do not fall under the Tarot, Lenormand or playing card systems, are usually classed as oracle cards. The symbols and meanings of oracle cards vary from deck to deck.

OSTEOMANCY: a form of casting divination that involves using bones, shells and other small items. The items are thrown down and their position interpreted by a diviner. (See Chapter 13.)

RUNES: a method of divination using 24 stones that depict runic symbols. Runes can be cast or randomly selected, and their meanings interpreted. (See Chapter 10.)

TAROT: a deck of 78 cards used for divination. (See Chapter 5.)

TASSEOMANCY: a method of divination that assigns special meaning to how tea leaves form in teacups. (See Chapter 9.)

LIST OF SYMBOLS
AND MEANINGS

Here is a handy, quick-reference guide to the most common and popular symbols for you to refer to in your readings. These descriptions are simplified to make it easy for you when you're starting out as a diviner. As you become more proficient, your understanding of symbols will develop and your readings will become more nuanced.

Once you learn the following symbolic meanings, you can apply them to other methods of divination. If symbols keep coming back to you, it's worth researching and investigating their divination meanings further.

ANIMALS

ALLIGATOR:
emotionally numb

ANT: industrious

BAT: long-lived

BIRDS: freedom-loving

BULL: sexually
frustrated

BUTTERFLY: frivolous

CAMEL: far-sighted

CAT: mystical

CATERPILLAR:
double-dealer

CHICKEN: gossip

COW: opulence

CRAB: intuitive

CROW: death

DOG: close friend

DOLPHIN: intelligent

DUCK: happy

EAGLE: perfectionist

FLAMINGO:
attention-seeking

FLEA: annoying

FLIES: sickly

FROG: confused

GOAT: promiscuous

GOLDFISH: investor

HEDGEHOG: old friend

HORSE: hard-working

HYENA: sadistic

KANGAROO: world traveller

LION: majestic

LOBSTER: cruel

MAGPIE: faithful

MONKEY: unevolved

MOUSE: disease

OSTRICH: quick

OTTER: inconsiderate

OWL: unlucky

PARROT: nosey

PIGEON: reliable

RABBIT: sexy

RHINOCEROS: overweight

SALMON: rich

SEAL: entertaining

SHARK: hurtful

SHEEP: playful

SNAIL: meticulous

SPIDER: wealthy

SQUIRREL: frugal

SWAN: loving

TURKEY: family-orientated

TURTLE: wise

VULTURE: scavenging

WASP: callous

WHALE: notable

WOLF: spiritual

WORM: opportunistic

ZEBRA: cosmopolitan

BODY

ARM: opportunities

BONE: life force

BREASTS: fertility

EAR: memory

EYE: intuition

FINGER: ideas

FOOT: strength

HAND: effort levels

HEAD: logic

LEGS: perseverance

MOUTH: health

NOSE: discoveries

PENIS: masculine side

VULVA: feminine side

FOOD

BREAD: assets

DAIRY: abundance

FRUIT: opportunities that expire quickly

MEAT: prosperity

SEAFOOD:
wealth and consumption

VEGETABLES:
opportunities that are open
to you for a long time

WATER: spirituality

HOME

ATTICS AND
BASEMENTS: old secrets

BASKET: rewards

BATH OR
SHOWER: renewal

BED: relaxation
(but sometimes sickness)

BLANKET: security

BUCKET: emotional
baggage

CANDLES: ritual,
sometimes habits

CARPET: routines

COT: broodiness

CURTAINS: privacy

CUTLERY: action

DOOR: opportunity

FENCE: safety

FOUNTAIN OR BIRD
BATH: social gatherings

GARDENING

TOOLS: assistance or ease ·

KITCHEN: survival instincts

LIVING ROOM:
sense of self

MAP: expedition

MIRROR: self-reflection

PAINTING: mastery

SEAT: observations

STAIRS OR
LADDER: developments

TOILET: re-establishment

NATURE

BEACH: reassurance

CAVE: house move

CROSSROADS: decisions

DESERT: financial loss

ECLIPSE: transformation
for good or evil

FIELD: new possibilities

FLOWERS: beauty

FOREST: family

ISLAND: isolation, loneliness

LAGOON: fantasies

MAZE OR LABYRINTH:
feeling trapped

OCEANS OR RIVER:
emotions and a chance
for change

PLANETS: new horizons

PLANTS: vitality
STAR: wishes
SUN: successes

WEATHER

AIR: intellect
CLOUDS: difficulty
FLOOD: life-changing events

FOG: confusion
HAIL: embarrassment
HEAT: passion
ICE: failure
RAIN: strong emotions
RAINBOW: reassurance
SNOW: unresolved issues
THUNDER: divine approval
WIND: one door closing, another opening

AUTHOR ACKNOWLEDGEMENTS

First of all, I would like to thank the spirits of my ancestors. Without their constant guidance I would not be where I am today. I would cease to exist. I am eternally grateful for everything they have done for me.

Secondly, I would like to thank my family, especially my mum and granny. Your never-ending support of my love of divination has made this book possible. Life would be very different without this support.

Thirdly, I am grateful for my baby, Candyce. You being such a good child made writing this book a lot easier! I love you, always.

I would also like to thank the love of my life, David, for listening to me bang on and on about this book. Thank you for always supporting my vision and believing in me unconditionally.

Most importantly, thank you to Elen for approaching me to write this book! You changed my life and I'm glad I took this opportunity.

Finally, I would like to thank the rest of the team at Laurence King. Working with you all has been a dream. Thank you for everything.